MORE THAN A TEA PARTY

A COLLECTION OF REGIONAL RECIPES FROM THE JUNIOR LEAGUE OF BOSTON

1989

The Junior League of Boston

The Junior League of Boston

ASK ME ABOUT THE JUNIOR LEAGUE OF BOSTON

The Junior League of Boston, Inc. is an organization of young women who demonstrate an interest in and commitment to volunteerism. Its purpose is educational and charitable. The Junior League of Boston's focus of efforts are divided into three areas of community need: Community Assistance and Education, Children and the Arts. Membership in the Junior League of Boston is open to women of all races, colors, religions, and national origins. There are 2,000 Provisional, Active and Sustainer members. The Junior League of Boston was founded in 1907 and incorporated as a non-profit organization in 1922.

For more information please write:
The Junior League of Boston, Inc.
117 Newbury Street
Boston, Massachusetts 02116

ISBN 0-9604156-1-0

For additional copies of *More Than a Tea Party—A Collection of Regional Recipes from The Junior League of Boston* please write:

MORE THAN A TEA PARTY
The Junior League of Boston, Inc.
117 Newbury Street
Boston, Massachusetts 02116

Include your return address with a check payable to The Junior League of Boston in the amount of $19.95 per book plus $2.00 postage and handling, $4.00 if ordering 2 or more. Massachusetts residents add $1.00 sales tax per book.

Printed by:
Hart Graphics
Austin, Texas

Junior League Cookbook Committee

Co-Chairmen
1987 – 1989

Minda H. Bradley
Patricia G. Carolan

Committee Members
1987 – 1989

Laurie Beneski
Pam Boyer
Wendy Chute
Dotty Corcoran
Ann Clemon Dewitt
Betsey Dobson
Lynn D. Donovan
Patricia C. Feige
Heather Holmes
  Floyd
Nancy Freedman
Karla Goodman
Jodi Harger
Ann Hartwell

Susan Hill
Ann Jackson
Dot S. Jacobson
Janet Kluczynski
Erin Lehman
Beverly N. Lochridge
Ann Marie Lynch
Heidi Maddrix
Kathleen Nakushian
Mary Ellen O'Donnell
Laurie Osgood
Cynthia Smithy
Liz Taggart
Margaret Webb

Recipe Testers
1987 – 1988

Becky Andrews
Gabrielle Bjornson
Patty Cadwgan
Dotty Corcoran
Joy Cornell
Mary Fish
Annie Freedman
Patricia Frolin
Ruth Georgevits
Terri Hale
Michelle Hanss
Barbara Hill
Sheeran Howard
Harriet Kinnett

Mary Kuhrtz
Gina Lloyd
Judy Mittleman
Laurie Osgood
Cynthia Payne
Betsy Regan
Nancy Sawyer
Emily Schmidt
Jill Staniar
Sharon Stolle
Anne Marie Vigeron
Julie Wade
Mary Ann Walter

Executive Liaisons

Amy McCreary 1987 – 1988
Pam Hulme 1988 – 1989

Back Cover, Boston and Freedom Trail Photography

Susan Fisher

SUSAN FISHER is a commerical photographer living in Boston, Massachusetts. Her work includes architectural, advertising and promotional photography. Before relocating to New England, Susan lived and worked primarily in Colorado. She plans to continue working on projects on the East Coast and in the West.

Front Cover Photograph

Conway Photography

Preface

The creation of *More Than A Tea Party, A Collection Of Regional Recipes From The Junior League Of Boston* began in 1986. It has been a thrilling venture, involving many league volunteers.

More Than A Tea Party is an outstanding collection of contemporary recipes that feature our regional Boston style and our local Massachusetts ingredients. Our legends, customs, and varied heritages are explored along the seventeen Freedom Trial stops, as you are taken on a guided culinary tour of Boston. The classic Boston dishes, including plenty of seafood and shellfish, grilled meats, hearty chowders, seasonal fruits and rich desserts are described in easy to follow directions.

All of the recipes presented here were submitted by the members of The Junior League of Boston and their friends unless otherwise credited. Each recipe is original, even as a variation of a well-known dish.

We encourage you to combine food items, borrow ideas, ingredients, or techniques to create a varied menu which is characterized by your own sense of cooking style.

More Than A Tea Party is more than a cookbook. It is one of the Junior League of Boston's main community fund-raising programs. The annual proceeds support more than thirty projects within the local community.

The development and final creation of *More Than A Tea Party, A Collection Of Regional Recipes From The Junior League Of Boston* has been a rewarding experience for us all.

The Cookbook Committee

Contents

The Freedom Trail

LEGEND

1. ~ State House and Archives
2. ~ Park Street Church
3. ~ Granary Burying Ground
4. ~ King's Chapel
5. ~ Franklin Statue
6. ~ Old South Meeting House
7. ~ Old Corner Book Store
8. ~ Old State House
9. ~ Faneuil Hall
10. ~ Quincy Market
11. ~ Paul Revere House
12. ~ Old North Church
13. ~ Copp's Hill Burying Ground
14. ~ Navy Yard ---"Old Ironsides"
15. ~ Bunker Hill Monument

11.

15.

Bartlett St.

Cross St.

Cedar St.

15.

Mt. Vernon St.

14.

Wallace Ct.

Chestnut St.

Cordis St.

Pleasant St.

Monument Av.

Soley St.

Bridge St.

Warren St.

Winthrop St.

Main St.

Monument St.

Park St.

Putnam St.

Ellwood St.

Harvard St.

Henley St.

Prescott

Chelsea St.

14.

Boston
Inner
Harbor

John F. Fitzgerald Exp'y

Charlestown Bridge

Front

North Washington St.

13.

MATHER
TOMB

12.

9.

Commercial St.

Charter St.

Foster St.

Causeway St.

N. Margin St.

Medford St.

Snowhill St.

13.

Hull St.

Sheafe St.

Tileston St.

12.

Unity St.

Newman

Hanover St.

Battery St.

Harris St.

Clark St.

Fleet St.

N. Bennet St.

Prince St.

Salutation St.

8.

3.

10.

10.

Noyes Pl.

Baldwin Pl.

Cooper St.

Wiget St.

Stillman St.

Morton

Salem St.

Tileston St.

Parmenter

Garden Ct.

Fleet & Lewis

Moon St.

Sun Ct.

North Street

11.

North Richmond

1.

4.

Cross

Hanover

Blackstone St.

93

6.

Congress St.

Union St.

North St.

Clinton St.

9.

10.

Chatham Row

Boston Massacre Marker

2.

Derne St.

Bowdoin St.

New Sudbury St.

Court St.

Court
Square

8.

State St.

Dane

1.

Joy Pl.

Joy St.

Beacon
Street

Park St.

Quaker Exchange

Bosworth St.

Province St.

Tremont St.

4.

5.

Water St.

2.

3.

7.

Spring Lane

Milk St.

Bromfield

Hamilton Pl.

6.

INFORMATION
KIOSK

Winter St.

5.

7.

Introduction

On a cold wintry day, December 16, 1773, a large group of colonists gathered outside the Old South Meeting House in protest against the landing of the cargoes of three tea-laden English ships at Griffin's Wharf in Boston Harbor. Samual Adams delivered a fiery address denouncing British tyranny and the hated tax on tea.

That night, ninety citizens secretly gathered at a nearby tavern and disguised themselves as Indians. Led by the vocal patriot, Samual Adams, the colonists swarmed onto the vessels and frightened the captains and crews below. Without a shot being fired, three hundred and forty-two chests of East Indian tea were broken open and thrown overboard. This marked the first open rebellion by the colonists and the first significant step leading to the Revolutionary War. It was more than just a tea party.

The Freedom Trail connects seventeen historic sites from the Boston Common to the Bunker Hill Monument bringing to life the historic path our early forefathers took to reach our independence from British rule.

In addition to the sites on the Freedom Trail, a replica of one of the three tea-laden ships from England is located at the Congress Street Bridge in Boston. The replica of the cargo ship, BEAVER, is open to the public year round. At 511 Atlantic Avenue, on the corner of Pearl Street, a bronze tablet marks the location of the now-landfilled Griffin's Wharf and the site of the Boston Tea Party.

Boston is rich with history. Come with us now and begin a most unusual culinary and historic tour of Boston.

Boston Common/Public Garden

Boston's Common was established in 1638 and is the oldest public park in America. It is located in the heart of Boston, outlined by Park, Tremont, Boylston, Beacon and Charles Streets. Today, it is the epicenter of our "Common-wealth," a favorite place for Bostonians to walk with friends, for children to play in cool fountains during the summer, and for all groups to enjoy outdoor concerts and gatherings. Across the way in the Public Garden, for a mere 90 cents, you can take a ride on a paddlewheel swanboat around one of the three original tiny ponds.

The land was once owned by the reclusive Reverend William Blackstone, who came to America as a missionary of the Church of England. He preferred "trading oysters with the Indians to trading conversation with his fellow countrymen," and preoccupied himself with his library, herd of goats and rose garden. All three endeavors prospered and it wasn't long before the Puritans, inhabiting Charlestown across the river, were drawn to the fertile "Shawmut Peninsula." They immediately renamed it Boston for their hometown in Lincolnshire, England.

Reverend Blackstone was not happy with his new neighbors and quickly bundled up his belongings and headed for Rhode Island. The Puritans, however, reimbursed him for his forty-five acres at six shillings per colonist, or about $150. The area was then proclaimed "common" property for the grazing of cattle and the training of militia.

The Puritans found a third use for this property: the punishment of colonists by stockade. As one of his first acts as Governor of the Commonwealth, John Winthrop had the stocks built on Boston Common to punish those citizens who were found committing such "terrible" crimes as eavesdropping, meddling, kissing in public, "sleeping in meeting" and the like. As it turned out, the very carpenter who built these stocks was the first man to be "installed" in them. Governor Winthrop thought he charged too much!

CHEESE

The invention of cheese, mythology tells us, is ascribed to Aristaeus, the son of Apollo by the nymph Cyrene. The very earliest references to this food go back nearly six thousand years. There are many references to it in the Bible. Cheese has been with us always, and new varieties are ever evolving, each with its own individual character. There are cheeses for every palate and occasion.

Cheese is made from many different milks, including goat, ewe, camel, water buffalo and cow. The flavor, texture and shape of cheese is as varied as the milk used to prepare it. The techniques to make cheese are only limited by man's lack of ingenuity.

All natural cheeses are divided into three basic types: soft, semihard and hard. There are fresh young cheeses, aged cheeses and cheeses with blue-veins. Some cheese is plain, others are flavored with smoke, peppercorns, garlic, herbs, spices, meats, vegetables, oils, nuts and other seasonings as well.

The benefits and pleasures of cheese are many. One of cheese's most endearing qualities is that it can stand almost alone and yet be so satisfying. Another is that cheese needs a minimum of preparation and yet is so elegant. Preparing a cheese repast takes practically no effort. Only imagination is needed for the presentation and serving of cheese. The ease of advanced preparation and the spectacle of presentation makes cheese perfectly suited to a large gathering or an intimate dinner.

Cheese can be served completely unadorned or embellished with a variety of fruits, breads, vegetables and nuts.

Do remember some very simple notes about cheeses:

- Cheese needs time to warm to room temperature and full flavor before serving. The time it takes to let a cheese reach room temperature varies with the solidity and size of the piece. As a gauge, allow approximately three hours for a half-pound wedge of natural Cheddar to come from the refrigerator to full taste.

- The best way to buy blue cheese is to sample it first. The texture should be creamy or firm depending on the type of cheese. The rind should not have cracks. The taste should be flavorful but not overly sharp or salty. A faint smell of ammonia means the cheese is over the hill.

- Some firm cheeses, such as Parmesan and Cheddar can be frozen. Cheese that has been frozen is best used for cooking, since the texture will become grainy.

- For the top-of-the-stove cooking, use moderate heat. High temperatures and long cooking toughen cheese and make it stringy.

Here are two simple but unusual serving suggestions:

Pineapple and Provolone

Place a one-inch thick crosswise slice of fresh unpeeled pineapple on top of a ½-inch thick slice of round smoky Italian provolone cheese. Mellow at room temperature at least 30 minutes. Carve into eight wedges to serve. Garnish with toasted coconut or lightly toasted pine nuts.

Danish Blue Cheese Smørrebrød

Spread thin slices of caraway light rye bread with softened unsalted butter then with a thin layer of a softened Danish Blue Cheese. Slice the bread into fingers and spoon tiny dollops of cherry preserves on top.

Smoked Salmon and Dill Torte

The famous swanboats of the Boston Public Garden have been a part of the city's rites of Spring since 1877.

The Paget family developed the idea for the boats and it has been a family-run business ever since.

Robert Paget was inspired in 1871 by the opera "Lohengrin." In the opera, Lohengrin saves princess Lisa by crossing a river being pulled by a swan.

2 packages (8 ounces each) cream cheese, softened

2 sticks unsalted butter, softened

1 tablespoon freshly grated lemon rind

1 tablespoon fresh lemon juice

½ cup finely chopped fresh dill

¼ pound smoked salmon or lox, finely chopped

¼ cup red caviar, divided (optional)

GARNISH:

Caviar

Sprigs of fresh dill

- Beat cream cheese and butter in medium bowl until light and fluffy.

- Add lemon rind and lemon juice.

- Divide into 2 bowls of ⅓ rd and ⅔ rds of mixture.

- Blend chopped dill well into the smaller mixture.

- Blend salmon into the larger mixture.

- Line a tall bowl with plastic wrap, leaving 2″ overhang.

- Pack salmon mixture firmly into lined bowl.

- Sprinkle ¼ cup caviar evenly over salmon mixture.

- Carefully spread dill and cheese mixture over caviar.

- Cover with plastic wrap overhang.

- Refrigerate 2 – 3 hours until firm.

- To serve, fold back plastic wrap, unmold torte onto serving plate. Carefully remove wrap.

- Garnish top with caviar and dill sprigs.

Cheddar Bites

2 sticks unsalted butter, softened

1 pound sharp Cheddar cheese, grated

1 large egg yolk

½ teaspoon cayenne pepper

2 teaspoons salt

2 cups all purpose flour

1 large egg white beaten with a pinch of salt

- Preheat oven to 375°F. Lightly butter a cookie sheet.

- In bowl of an electric mixer or in food processor, blend the butter and cheese until smooth.

- Add the egg yolk, cayenne and salt and blend well.

- Add the flour and mix until it forms a soft dough.

- Working in batches, pack the dough in a cookie press fitted with a decorative tip and press into decorative mounds two inches apart on the prepared cookie sheet.

- Brush the tops with the egg white glaze and bake the mounds in the middle of preheated oven for 10 minutes, until puffed and lightly golden.

- Transfer the cheddar bites with a spatula to racks.

- The cheddar bites may be served warm or at room temperature.

90 CRACKERS

Note: They will keep in an airtight container for 3 days or frozen. To reheat, place in preheated 300°F. oven for 5 minutes.

These addicting cheese crackers can be made in a variety of shapes to suit the occasion or season.

Mini Cheese Soufflés

A tasty hot cheese hors d'oeuvre that is frozen before baking. It can go from freezer to oven anytime that a quick hors d'oeuvre is needed.

½ loaf rye bread

1 package (3 ounces) cream cheese

¼ pound Gruyère or Swiss cheese, grated

1 stick butter

2 egg whites, stiffly beaten

- Preheat oven to 450°F. Line a cookie sheet with wax paper.

- Remove crust from bread and cut the loaf into 1" squares.

- Melt cream cheese, Gruyère and butter in a double boiler until creamy.

- Remove from heat and fold in egg whites.

- Dip bread cubes into mixture and transfer to the prepared cookie sheet. Freeze.

- Store squares in an airtight plastic bag in the freezer.

- Bake for approximately 8 minutes. Serve immediately.

Note: Double cheese mixture to use whole loaf of bread.

Flaming Cheese

An elegant cheese hors d'oeuvre that is quick to assemble and the ingredients can be easily adjusted to suit the size of the group.

Kasseri is a hard, grating cheese from Greece, made from ewe's milk.

1 pound Kasseri cheese

¼ cup brandy

1 pound pita bread, cut in triangles, or 1 loaf sourdouqh bread

- Preheat oven to 350°F.

- Shred cheese onto an oven-proof dish or platter.

- Melt cheese in oven until bubbly.

- Remove from oven and place dish on heat-proof tray.

- Pour 3 tablespoons of brandy on cheese.

- Ignite remaining tablespoon of brandy and pour over cheese.

- Serve flaming, with pita bread triangles or sourdough bread chunks.

Roquefort-Stuffed Brie

2 small rounds of ripe Brie,
   chilled

1 stick unsalted butter,
   softened

¼ pound Roquefort cheese,
   room temperature

1½ tablespoons cognac

¼ cup chopped pecans

GARNISH:

Pecan halves

- Keep Brie chilled while preparing stuffing.
- Combine butter, Roquefort and cognac until smooth.
- Add chopped pecans and combine.
- Cut cold Brie rounds in half horizontally.
- Carefully separate them and spread stuffing on the bottom layers.
- Replace the top layers on the Brie rounds.
- Garnish with pecan halves.

Camembert Almondine

1 young Camembert, chilled

Unsalted butter

Brown sugar

Slivered almonds, toasted

- Preheat oven to 350°F.
- Slice off the top of the cheese rind.
- Place the cheese in a heat-proof serving dish. Dot the top with unsalted butter and sprinkle generously with brown sugar.
- Bake for 10 – 15 minutes until the cheese softens in the center.
- Quickly brown the cheese under broiler to caramelize the sugar.
- Sprinkle with toasted almonds and serve immediately.
- Serve with crackers or crusty bread rounds.

An interesting contrast in flavors. The Brie is easy to assemble and may be done so a day in advance of serving.

Any size Brie works perfectly, just adjust the amount of filling.

Liptauer

Liptauer can also be served in a hollowed-out round loaf of rye bread. Use the diced pieces of rye bread in place of crackers.

1 tablespoon instant minced onion

2 teaspoons dry mustard

2 tablespoons warm water

1 stick butter or margarine, softened

1 package (8 ounces) cream cheese, softened

2 anchovy fillets, finely minced

1 teaspoon capers, finely minced

1 tablespoon caraway seed

White pepper, to taste

GARNISH:

Fresh parsley

Paprika

- Mix onion and mustard with 2 tablespoons warm water. Let stand 10 minutes.

- In small mixing bowl, cream butter. Gradually add cream cheese, blending well.

- To creamed mixture add onion-mustard mixture, anchovies, capers, caraway seed and white pepper.

- Mix together thoroughly and pack into a 2 cup bowl or glass. Chill until firm.

- Garnish with parsley and paprika.

Camembert Pepper Glaze

This elegant Camembert is perfect for a cocktail buffet. It can be easily prepared in advance.

Serve a sampling of miniature (4 ounces) Camemberts with varied colored pepper jellies (red, yellow or green) swirled through the tops for a festive presentation.

1 young Camembert, chilled

6 – 8 ounces horseradish jelly or horseradish-pepper jelly

- Preheat oven to 350°F.
- Slice off the top of the cheese rind.
- Place the cheese in a heat-proof serving dish. Spread the jelly over top of cheese.
- Bake for 15 – 20 minutes until the cheese softens in the center.
- Serve with melba toast or crusty French bread.

Boston Public Garden

Park Street Church

The State House

Prominently situated at the top of Beacon Hill, the last remaining of Old Boston's seven hills, is the new State House. The building was designed in 1798 by Boston's renowned architect, Charles Bulfinch, and underwent a series of expansions through 1917. Its famous golden dome was originally cast in copper by Paul Revere in 1802, gilded in 1861 and topped with 23½ carat gold leaf in 1874. The dome's present-day value stands at more than 2 million dollars. During World War II, the dome was painted gray to prevent easy detection of Boston by the Germans. On top of the dome is a pine cone representing the timberlands of Maine. Maine was part of Massachusetts at the time of construction.

The State House was built upon the land that was owned by John Hancock's family and is situated just to the right of what was once the old Hancock mansion. Bulfinch's plan for the young Commonwealth's capitol was based on London's Somerset House, a monumental neo-Palladian government building situated on the Thames. This was the original building. In 1898, a hundred years later, a new section was added to the back of the State House to accommodate the offices of legislators and administrators. In 1917, two wings were added on either side of the main structure expanding the State House to its present size and stature.

The archives, located in the State House, contain many original documents, such as the Massachusetts Constitution of 1780 and Bradford's History of Plimouth Plantation.

Boston Beer Boiled Shrimp

These sensational shrimp make a great hors d'oeuvre or a satisfying luncheon entrée.

When buying shrimp, it can be useful to know that 2 – 2½ pounds of shrimp in the shell equals about 1 pound of cooked shelled shrimp .

1 – 1½ pounds medium shrimp in shells

1 can (12 ounces) beer

½ teaspoon thyme

½ teaspoon dry mustard

1½ tablespoons chopped fresh parsley

1 garlic clove, minced

1½ teaspoons salt

1 bay leaf

½ teaspoon chopped onion

- Place shrimp, beer, thyme, mustard, parsley, garlic, salt, bay leaf and onion in a large pot and cover.
- Bring to a boil and reduce heat immediately.
- Simmer 3 minutes. The shrimp should be pink.
- Drain and cool shrimp, peel and devein.
- Chill and serve with cocktail sauce.

Pesto Hots

Fresh basil may be frozen or dried. To freeze, wrap the leaves in an airtight plastic bag and place in the freezer. To dry, hang the basil plant upside down and when the leaves are dry, crumble them and place in an airtight container.

½ cup slivered fresh basil leaves

½ cup freshly grated Parmesan cheese

1 garlic clove, minced

6 tablespoons mayonnaise

1 French bread baguette, sliced into ¼" thick rounds

- Preheat broiler.
- Stir together basil, cheese, garlic and mayonnaise.
- Arrange bread slices on cookie sheet.
- Place cookie sheet under broiler and toast one side.
- Remove from oven, turn bread slices over and spread each slice with a generous teaspoonful of mixture.
- Return to broiler. Cook until bubbly and lightly browned.

2 DOZEN

Back Bay Pâté

3 garlic cloves, crushed

4 tablespoons butter

1 pound chicken livers

¼ cup sliced onion

¼ cup heavy cream

2 tablespoons dry sherry

½ teaspoon salt

½ teaspoon celery salt

¼ teaspoon freshly ground black pepper

2 eggs, hard boiled

- Sauté crushed garlic in butter.

- Add chicken livers until just tender and no longer pink inside.

- Add onion a few minutes before livers are cooked.

- Cool mixture.

- Transfer liver mixture with cream, sherry, salt, celery salt and pepper to blender or food processor and purée until smooth.

- Add eggs and continue to blend until smooth.

- Refrigerate several hours before serving.

- Slice the pâté with a serrated knife and serve with any of the following condiments:
      capers
      thin slices of Bermuda onion
      Dijon mustard
      sliced tomatoes
      cornichons

Note: *Pâté can be frozen.*

Softened pâté can also be spread or piped onto apple slices, pear slices, bread or toast.

Dijon Dip with Fresh Crudités

When making a mayonnaise it is very important to add the oil ever so slowly to the eggs. You are actually attempting to coat the droplets of oil with egg to keep them in a creamy suspension.

Should your mayonnaise curdle, beat a new egg yolk in a separate bowl and add a few droplets of oil until it is very thick. Then, very slowly add this to your curdled mayonnaise.

2 cups fresh Brussels sprouts

1 cup fresh baby carrots, peeled

1 cup fresh pea pods

1 cup fresh green beans, trimmed

1 pound fresh asparagus

1 small red cabbage

2 egg yolks

1 tablespoon red wine vinegar

3 tablespoons Dijon mustard

1 teaspoon dill

1 cup vegetable oil

- Bring large pot of salted water to a boil.
- Blanch Brussels sprouts, carrots, pea pods, beans and asparagus in turn, using the same pot of water.
- Transfer each vegetable when done to a bowl of ice water.
- Drain all vegetables thoroughly, making sure they are dry.
- Hollow core of the cabbage.
- Combine egg yolks, vinegar, mustard and dill in bowl of food processor.
- With motor running, slowly add oil, blending to form a mayonnaise.
- Shut off motor and scrape dip into a bowl.
- Cover and refrigerate until ready to serve.
- To serve, pour dip into cabbage and place on a platter.
- Arrange vegetables around cabbage.

Mushroom Turnovers

1 package (8 ounces) cream cheese, softened

1½ cups all purpose flour

1 stick plus 3 tablespoons butter, softened, divided

½ pound mushrooms, minced

1 large onion, minced

¼ cup sour cream

¾ teaspoon salt

¼ teaspoon thyme

2 tablespoons all purpose flour

1 egg, beaten

- In large bowl at medium speed, beat cream cheese, flour and 1 stick butter until smooth.
- Shape dough into ball and wrap. Chill 1 hour.
- In 10" skillet over medium heat, cook mushrooms and onions in 3 tablespoons of butter until tender. Stir occasionally.
- Stir in sour cream, salt, thyme and 2 tablespoons of flour. Set aside.
- Preheat oven to 450°F.
- On floured surface with floured rolling pin, thinly roll out half of dough.
- With floured 2¾" cookie cutter, cut out as many circles as possible. Repeat with remaining dough.
- Place teaspoon of mushroom mixture on one half of each dough circle.
- Brush edges of circles with beaten egg.
- Fold dough over filling, and with a fork, press edges firmly together to seal. Prick tops.
- Brush turnovers with remaining egg.
- Place turnovers on ungreased cookie sheet.
- Bake for 12 – 14 minutes, until golden.

3½ DOZEN

Note: Turnovers can be prepared in advance and frozen before baking.

Hors d'oeuvres are traditionally served with drinks prior to the main entrée, or they may be combined to create a varied and satisfying meal.

Barbecued Clams

A perfect grill side hors d'oeuvre.

Pair with PESTO HOTS when basil is abundant in the garden.

36 clams, suitable for steaming, scrubbed

1 stick butter

2 garlic cloves, minced

1 tablespoon minced fresh chives

2 tablespoons minced fresh parsley

1 French bread baguette, sliced into ½" thick rounds

- Place clams in a bowl adjacent to barbecue.

- Set grill 4" above a solid bed of coals.

- In a 2-quart saucepan, combine butter, garlic, chives and parsley. Place on grill slightly away from heat so butter melts without burning.

- Set each clam on grill until it begins to open, approximately 5 minutes.

- Turn clams over and continue to cook until clams pop wide open, 5 – 10 minutes more.

- Protecting fingers with napkin, hold opened clams over butter pan to drain clam juice into butter.

- To eat, spear clam with fork, dip into butter mixture and eat with bread slices dipped into butter mixture.

Hot Lobster Dip

4 packages (8 ounces each) cream cheese

24 ounces frozen langostinos, thawed and drained

⅔ cup dry white wine

2 teaspoons dry mustard

⅔ cup mayonnaise

1 teaspoon horseradish

1 teaspoon onion salt

Pinch of garlic powder

- In a saucepan, combine cream cheese, langostinos, wine, mustard, mayonnaise, horseradish, onion salt and garlic powder and heat. Thin with more wine if needed.

- Serve with crusty French bread or sourdough bread.

Note: Freezes very well. Reheat over low heat or in a double boiler.

Bacon Onion Tomato Bites

36 cherry tomatoes

1¼ pounds bacon

8 green onions, minced

⅓ cup mayonnaise

Freshly ground black pepper, to taste

GARNISH:

Parsley sprigs

- Slice off bottom end of tomato (not stem end, so they will stand up). Hollow out seeds and place upside down on paper towels to drain.

- Fry bacon until crisp, drain well and crumble.

- Mix bacon with green onion, mayonnaise and a grind or two of pepper.

- Stuff tomatoes and chill for 45 minutes.

- Garnish with parsley sprigs.

Langostinos are a type of lobster shipped to the United States frozen from South Africa and Europe. They have no claws and most of the meat is from the tail.

A cherry tomato is easily hollowed out with a melon-ball scoop.

Patriot's Pâté

A simple variation on the traditional potted meat.

1 pound chicken livers, well rinsed

½ pound bacon, diced

1 large onion, chopped

4 garlic cloves, chopped

4 bay leaves

1 teaspoon salt

¼ teaspoon cayenne pepper

2 tablespoons Worcestershire sauce

6 cups water

½ teaspoon freshly grated nutmeg

1 teaspoon yellow mustard

⅛ teaspoon ground cloves

- Place livers in a large saucepan with bacon.
- Add the onion, garlic, bay leaves, salt, red pepper, Worcestershire sauce and water.
- Bring to a boil, reduce heat and simmer, covered for 20 minutes.
- Drain the livers. Discard bay leaves.
- Place livers and drained ingredients in the bowl of a food processor.
- Add to this mixture nutmeg, mustard and cloves.
- Process until smooth.
- Transfer the liver mixture to a crock, decorative mold or individual ramekins.
- Refrigerate covered until ready to use.
- Serve with cornichons and grainy mustard as accompaniments.

Note: *Pâté can be kept in the refrigerator for one week or frozen for up to one month.*

Shrimp Rémoulade

2 pounds shrimp, cleaned, boiled and chilled

1 bunch green onions

2 stalks celery, divided

1 tablespoon fresh parsley

3 tablespoons creole-style mustard

2 tablespoons paprika

1¼ teaspoons salt

½ teaspoon freshly ground black pepper

⅓ cup white wine vinegar

2 tablespoons fresh lemon juice

¾ cup olive oil

Cayenne pepper to taste

Romaine lettuce leaves, washed and separated

- Coarsely chop green onions and 1½ stalks celery, reserving ½ stalk.

- In blender or food processor, purée green onions, chopped celery, parsley, mustard, paprika, salt, pepper, vinegar, lemon juice, oil and cayenne pepper.

- Finely mince reserved celery and add to the purée.

- Cover and refrigerate.

- Place chilled shrimp on individual Romaine leaves and cover with the rémoulade.

Note: This recipe can be easily multiplied.

Small leaves of Radicchio can be used as a colorful bed for the shrimp.

Spicy Stuffed Mushrooms

These are a very zesty and cheesy version of the traditional stuffed mushroom, made entirely in the microwave oven.

24 bite-size mushrooms

5 slices bacon, chopped

½ cup minced green onion

1 teaspoon salt

½ teaspoon freshly ground black pepper

¼ teaspoon savory

6 drops hot red pepper sauce

2 tablespoons all purpose flour

½ cup heavy cream

⅓ cup shredded Cheddar cheese

- Wash mushrooms, remove stems and chop stems finely.

- Microwave mushroom caps, uncovered, on a plate in single layer on medium-high for 1 minute.

- Microwave bacon on microwave-safe paper towels for 2 – 3 minutes until crisp.

- Mix mushroom stems, onion, salt, pepper, savory and pepper sauce in a microwave-safe bowl.

- Microwave 3 minutes, uncovered, on high until onion is soft, stirring twice.

- Add flour and cream to vegetable mixture and cook in microwave 3 minutes on medium-high, stirring twice.

- Fill each mushroom cap with prepared mixture, and place caps around outer edge of microwave plate.

- Top each cap with a sprinkle of cheese. Microwave 1 minute on medium until cheese is melted.

Endive Spirals

1 package (8 ounces) cream cheese, softened

½ cup cottage cheese

¼ cup minced green onions

¼ cup minced parsley

2 garlic cloves, minced

2 teaspoons thyme

Salt and freshly ground black pepper, to taste

6 Belgian endives

- Combine cream cheese, cottage cheese, green onions, parsley, garlic, thyme, salt and pepper.
- Separate the leaves of the endive and wipe clean.
- Starting with the innermost leaves, spread the cheese mixture on the leaves and re-form the endives as each leaf is coated with the cheese mixture.
- Chill the endives, tightly wrapped in plastic wrap for one hour or until the filling is firm.
- Cut the endives crosswise into ½″ slices and arrange on a serving tray.

Belgian endive has a bitter flavor and is frequently used raw in appetizers or cooked as a vegetable. Choose heads which are closed and pale yellow in color.

Curried Crabmeat Dip

13 ounces crabmeat (fresh, frozen or canned), flaked

2 packages (8 ounces each) cream cheese, softened

6 tablespoons mayonnaise

½ teaspoon salt

¼ teaspoon curry powder

2 tablespoons grated onion

1 tablespoon fresh lemon juice

1 teaspoon Worcestershire sauce

4 dashes hot pepper sauce

½ cup almonds, chopped

- In a mixing bowl, combine crabmeat, cream cheese, mayonnaise, salt, curry powder, onion, lemon juice, Worcestershire sauce, hot pepper sauce and almonds.
- Refrigerate, covered, overnight for flavors to blend.
- Serve with toast, French bread or crackers.

Biscuit cutters can be used to vary the shape of slices of toast, bread or even cucumber slices.

Chinatown Mini Egg Rolls

Chinese mustard is prepared by mixing a little water or vinegar with powdered mustard. If it is too fiery for your taste, tone it down by mixing in a little olive oil or vegetable oil.

1 cup finely chopped cooked shrimp

1½ cups fresh bean sprouts

1 cup minced celery

1 cup finely chopped green onions

1 can (6½ ounces) water chestnuts, drained and chopped

1 tablespoon vegetable oil

1 tablespoon smooth peanut butter

1 teaspoon salt

⅛ teaspoon freshly ground black pepper

⅛ teaspoon Chinese Five Spice Powder

2 packages of egg roll wrappers

1 teaspoon cornstarch

Vegetable oil for frying

GARNISH:

Hot mustard

Sweet and sour sauce

- Mix together shrimp, bean sprouts, celery, green onion, water chestnuts, oil, peanut butter, salt, pepper and Five Spice Powder.

- Cut wrappers into quarters.

- Place 1 teaspoon of filling in one of the corners.

- Lift the corner and put the point under the filling.

- Fold over the two edges and continue rolling.

- Moisten the end with a little water mixed with cornstarch to seal.

- Fry in hot vegetable oil until golden, about 2 minutes on each side.

- Drain on paper towels.

- Serve with hot mustard and sweet and sour sauce.

Note: Egg rolls can be frozen and reheated at 350°F.

HOT SOUPS, CHOWDERS AND STEWS

Park Street Church

On the corner of Tremont and Park Streets, just across the way from Boston Common, is the Park Street Church. Built by Peter Banner in 1809, this grand edifice with its towering steeple was considered by the Boston novelist Henry James to be "the most interesting mass of brick and mortar in America". Interesting indeed, for this Congregational church, which is still in use today, was the site of many fiery oratories and historical firsts.

In Park Street Church on July 4, 1829, the famous abolitionist and publisher, William Lloyd Garrison, gave his first public anti-slavery speech. Here in 1831, the first notes of Samuel Francis Smith's song "America" were sung out by school children in honor of that year's Independence Day celebration. In 1895, the Church experienced the effects of the country's very first subway system. While digging the tunnel for the subway, a workman broke through a water main which flooded the Church right in the middle of the minister's sermon.

The corner of the Boston Common opposite the Park Street Church is known as "Brimstone Corner". The area is so called not only because of the fiery speeches and sermons issued from the Church, but also for the load of brimstone or sulphur (used for gun powder) stored in the basement of the Park Street Church during the War of 1812.

Smoked Fish and Dill Stew

A hearty stew with a mellow smoky flavor. Serve with a simple green salad and crusty bread.

If finnan haddie is not available fresh, ask the fish market if they have it frozen.

1 pound smoked haddock (finnan haddie)

4 cups chicken broth

¼ pound bacon

1 onion, chopped

2 tablespoons all purpose flour

4 red potatoes, cut into ½" wedges

Freshly ground black pepper

¼ pound green beans, trimmed and cut into 1" pieces

1 cup whipping cream

¼ cup chopped fresh dill

- Place haddock in a large saucepan with broth.
- Cook, covered, over medium heat just until the broth starts to bubble.
- Reduce heat and simmer 8 minutes or until fish flakes easily.
- Using a spatula, transfer fish to a platter and reserve 3 cups stock in a separate bowl. Set aside.
- Cut bacon into 1" pieces and cook in a large skillet until crisp. Remove bacon.
- Cook onion in bacon fat until soft.
- Push onion to one side of pan and whisk in flour until bubbly.
- Gradually whisk in the reserved stock and bring to a boil.
- Add potatoes and pepper.
- Cover and simmer 5 minutes.
- Add beans, cover and simmer 5 to 10 minutes.
- Stir in cream and cook until very hot. Do not boil.
- Flake fish in large pieces, removing any bones.
- Gently stir fish, bacon and dill into stew.
- Cook just until haddock is heated through. Serve immediately.

4 SERVINGS

Red Pepper Soup

5 large sweet red peppers, cleaned and julienned

4 tablespoons butter

4 cups beef broth

Madeira, to taste

2 egg yolks

½ – 1 cup heavy cream

Cayenne pepper, to taste

GARNISH:

Julienned red pepper

- In large pot, sauté peppers briefly in butter to soften slightly.

- Add beef broth and simmer until peppers are quite soft.

- Purée peppers. Return to pan and reheat.

- Add Madeira to taste.

- Mix egg yolks with 4 tablespoons cream.

- Add a little hot soup to eggs, whisking constantly.

- Whisk the egg mixture into remaining hot soup.

- Add the remaining cream slowly to the hot soup, using the amount needed to reach desired thickness.

- Season gently with cayenne. Serve garnished with julienned pepper.

6 SERVINGS

Note: Do not substitute bouillon cubes for the beef broth. They are too salty.

Simple, yet beautiful. Intense color and flavor.

A dollop of sour cream makes an elegant garnish.

Leek and Potato Soup

A mellow and creamy soup that is very easy to prepare.

Garnish with ribbons of spinach.

6 leeks, washed

3 potatoes

1 bay leaf

1 tablespoon sage

3 tablespoons butter

2 tablespoons flour

2 cups milk

Salt and freshly ground black pepper, to taste

- Chop leeks, including some green part. Peel and cut up potatoes.

- Simmer leeks and potatoes in 3 cups lightly salted water with bay leaf and sage.

- When vegetables are tender, remove bay leaf and purée, using all the liquid.

- Make a very thin béchamel sauce with the butter, flour and milk seasoned with salt and pepper.

- Gradually incorporate the sauce with the purée of vegetables. Blend well.

- Heat through and serve.

6 – 8 SERVINGS

Note: Can be prepared ahead and gently reheated.

Pumpkin Almond Bisque

2 tablespoons butter

3 tablespoons chopped celery

3 tablespoons chopped onion

2 cups canned pumpkin

1 tablespoon tomato paste

2 tablespoons almond paste

3 cups chicken stock

1½ cups light cream

1 teaspoon freshly grated nutmeg

1 teaspoon white pepper

3 tablespoons almond liqueur

Salt, to taste

GARNISH:

Toasted pumpkin or sunflower seeds

- In heavy saucepan, melt butter over medium heat.

- Add celery and onions and simmer 5 minutes.

- Add pumpkin, tomato paste and almond paste. Blend well until smooth.

- Add chicken stock and simmer 30 minutes.

- Blend cream into soup, cooking until hot.

- Season with nutmeg, pepper, almond liqueur and salt.

- Garnish individual servings with seeds. Serve immediately.

6 SERVINGS

Note: *Cannot be prepared in advance or frozen. Do not cook covered or in microwave. Can be halved or doubled.*

Pumpkin never tasted so elegant!

To toast pumpkin seeds, rinse seeds and place on a buttered cookie sheet. Bake at 350°F. for 10 minutes or until golden. Sprinkle with salt.

Winter Cauliflower Cheese Soup

A creamy soup to serve on a cold snowy night.

Garnish with shredded red or green pepper or carrot for a splash of color.

3 cups cubed potatoes

3½ cups cauliflowerets, divided

1 cup peeled and chopped carrots

4 medium garlic cloves, minced

1 cup chopped onion

1 teaspoon salt

5 cups chicken stock or water

1½ cups grated Cheddar cheese

¾ cup milk

½ teaspoon dill

¼ teaspoon dry mustard

Freshly ground black pepper, to taste

2 tablespoons butter

¾ cup buttermilk

GARNISH:

Chopped green onions

Grated Cheddar cheese

- In a large pot, combine potatoes, 2 cups cauliflowerets, carrots, garlic, onion, salt and chicken stock.

- Bring soup to a boil, reduce heat, cover and simmer 15 minutes.

- Remove soup from heat and cool 10 minutes.

- Purée soup in a blender or food processor until smooth.

- Return puréed soup to the pot and heat gently.

- Whisk in grated cheese, milk, dill, mustard and pepper.

- Sauté remaining 1½ cups cauliflowerets in butter. Add to soup.

- Just before serving, whisk in buttermilk and ladle into warmed soup bowls.

- Garnish with chopped green onions and grated Cheddar cheese. Serve immediately.

6 SERVINGS

Exotic Mushroom Stew

1 pound small red potatoes, peeled, sliced in ½″ wedges

4 tablespoons unsalted butter

3 cups exotic wild mushrooms, at least 2 varieties of the following: shiitake, oyster, chanterelles, morels, etc., quartered

1 very small red onion, halved, then thinly sliced

1 can (14 ounces) chicken broth or stock

1 cup heavy cream

1 cup light cream

½ teaspoon sea salt

¼ teaspoon white pepper

¼ teaspoon marjoram

¼ teaspoon thyme

½ teaspoon chervil

GARNISH:

Chopped fresh chervil or parsley

- In medium saucepan, simmer potatoes until just tender, approximately 15 minutes. Drain and keep warm.

- In another medium saucepan, melt butter.

- Add mushrooms and sauté over low heat for 10 minutes, stirring gently.

- Add onion to mushrooms and cook over low heat until translucent, approximately 5 minutes.

- Add chicken stock to mushroom and onions. Simmer 20 minutes.

- Add creams, salt, pepper, marjoram, thyme, chervil and potatoes. Simmer 10 minutes until heated through. Do not boil.

- Serve garnished with chopped chervil.

6 SERVINGS

Note: Can be reheated gently over low heat.

A very unusual and delicious stew.

If fresh morels are not available, substitute dried morels. To reconstitute dried morels, add two tablespoons of apple brandy to water. This removes any harshness in the taste of the morels.

If using dried shiitake or black mushrooms soak them in warm water for 30 minutes to reconstitute them before adding to the stew.

Hearty Green and Gold Soup

Hearty and healthy.

Serve with fresh garlic croutons.

1 medium butternut squash, seeded, peeled and cut into 1" squares

2 cups cubed potatoes

2 cans (10¾ ounces each) chicken broth

1½ cups finely chopped carrots

1 cup chopped leek (one leek)

3 tablespoons butter

2½ cups milk

½ teaspoon basil

1 teaspoon freshly grated nutmeg

¼ teaspoon salt

¼ teaspoon freshly ground black pepper

1 package (10 ounces) frozen peas

- In a 4-quart pan, combine squash, potatoes and broth.
- Bring to boil and cover. Reduce heat and simmer 10 – 20 minutes or until vegetables are tender.
- Purée vegetables and liquid by thirds in blender. Return puréed mixture to pan.
- Sauté carrots and leek in butter until tender, approximately 10 minutes. Stir into purée.
- Stir in milk, basil, nutmeg, salt, pepper and frozen peas.
- Heat to boiling, reduce heat and simmer uncovered about 5 minutes.
- Serve immediately.

10 SERVINGS

Note: A light soup, this creation has only 200 calories per serving.

New England Clam Chowder

2 ounces salt pork, minced*

1 cup finely diced onions

2 tablespoons all purpose flour

4 cups clam broth**

2 cups water

3 cups peeled and cubed potatoes

1¼ cups chopped fresh clams***

2 pints light cream

2 tablespoons butter

Salt and freshly ground black pepper, to taste.

- In large saucepan, cook salt pork until crisp and light brown, stirring often.

- Add onions and cook, stirring, until wilted.

- Sprinkle with flour.

- Add clam broth, water and potatoes and stir.

- Bring to boil, then simmer for 20 minutes.

- Add clams and simmer 5 – 10 minutes more.

- Stir in cream and butter.

- Add salt and pepper to taste.

- Simmer on very low heat a few minutes more until heated through. Do not boil.

10 SERVINGS

  * Bacon can be substituted for salt pork.
 ** Store purchased.
*** Seafood stores and some markets sell fresh, chopped clams. Alternately, clean 24 chowder clams to remove sand. Place clams in large kettle with ¾ cup water and steam until they open, approximately 5 – 10 minutes. Do not overcook. Remove clams from shells and chop.

Cream of Artichoke Soup

An artichoke lover's dream come true. This vegetable salad soup makes a hearty hot meal.

2 tablespoons unsalted butter

½ cup chopped carrots

½ cup chopped onions

½ cup chopped celery

½ cup chopped mushrooms

2 tablespoons all purpose flour

1 cup chicken broth

2 cans (8½ ounces each) artichoke hearts, undrained, reserving 2 hearts

1 bay leaf

¾ teaspoon salt

½ teaspoon freshly ground black pepper

¼ teaspoon thyme

¼ teaspoon oregano

1 cup whipping cream

GARNISH:

Artichoke hearts

- Melt butter. Add carrots, onions, celery and mushrooms and sauté until soft.

- Add flour and cook, stirring.

- Stir in broth and artichoke hearts with juice.

- Add bay leaf, salt, pepper, thyme and oregano and stir.

- Increase heat to medium and simmer 30 minutes, stirring occasionally.

- Remove from heat and purée in food processor or blender. Return to pan.

- Whip cream until frothy and blend into soup.

- Heat through and serve.

- Garnish with quartered reserved artichoke hearts.

6 SERVINGS

Note: Can be prepared in advance, but add cream just before serving. Freezes well. Can be halved or doubled.

Squash, Leek and Watercress Soup

4 tablespoons unsalted butter

6 leeks, white part only, chopped

3 pounds yellow summer squash, chopped

2 quarts chicken stock

Dash of hot red pepper sauce

Salt and freshly ground black pepper, to taste

2 bunches watercress, stems removed

GARNISH:

½ cup sour cream

8 pieces thinly sliced squash

Sprigs of watercress

- Melt butter in heavy large saucepan over medium-low heat.

- Add leeks and cook until tender, stirring occasionally, about 10 minutes.

- Add chopped squash and stir for 4 minutes.

- Add chicken stock and simmer until squash is tender, about 15 minutes.

- Add pepper sauce and season with salt and pepper to taste.

- Add watercress and simmer 2 minutes.

- Purée soup in blender or food processor.

- Ladle into bowls, swirl in 1 tablespoon of sour cream and garnish with sliced squash and watercress sprig.

8 SERVINGS

Note: Best made 1 day ahead, refrigerated and reheated just before serving.

A beautiful spring green soup that has a silky smooth texture and a subtle flavor.

Asparagus and Crab Bisque

*When choosing
asparagus at the market
look for tips that are firm
and tight, not frayed, and
stalks which show no
signs of drying or
shriveling.*

1¼ pounds fresh asparagus,
   washed with thick ends
   cut off

1 small red onion, diced

2 cups chicken broth

2 tablespoons butter

2 tablespoons flour

6 ounces fresh crabmeat,
   shelled, or 6.5 ounce can of
   frozen crabmeat, rinsed
   and picked over

1 cup light cream or half and
   half

2 tablespoons sherry

Salt and freshly ground
   black pepper, to taste

GARNISH:

Asparagus tips

- In medium frying pan, cook asparagus for 4 – 5 minutes. Cut the tips off to use as garnish and reserve.

- Place asparagus, onion and chicken broth in saucepan. Boil for 5 minutes. Let cool.

- Purée asparagus mixture in food processor and set aside.

- Melt butter and blend in flour in large saucepan.

- Add the asparagus mixture and cook, stirring, for 5 minutes.

- Add crabmeat, cream and sherry. Heat, do not boil.

- Season to taste with salt and pepper.

- Pour soup in warmed soup bowls. Garnish each bowl with the reserved asparagus tips.

4 SERVINGS

Note: Shrimp can be substituted for the crabmeat for a different taste.

Pumpkin Soup

1½ cups firmly packed white bread crumbs

1 pumpkin, approximately 7 pounds

6 – 8 tablespoons butter

Salt

⅔ cup finely minced onion

Pinch of freshly grated nutmeg

½ teaspoon ground sage

½ cup grated Swiss cheese

3 – 4 cups chicken broth

½ cup heavy cream

1 bay leaf

Chopped fresh parsley

Pumpkins have been growing in America for over 5000 years. They are indigenous to the Western hemisphere and were completely unknown in Europe before the time of Columbus.

- Spread bread crumbs on baking sheet and let them dry out in a 300°F. oven for approximately 15 minutes, stirring occasionally.

- With a knife, cut a cover out of the top of the pumpkin. Using a metal spoon, scrape out and discard all of the seeds and stringy fiber from the cover and inside of the pumpkin.

- Rub inside of the pumpkin with 1 tablespoon butter and sprinkle lightly with salt.

- Preheat oven to 400°F.

- Melt 6 tablespoons butter and sauté onions for 8 – 10 minutes over low heat.

- Stir in bread crumbs and cook slowly 2 – 3 minutes.

- Stir in the nutmeg and sage. Remove from heat and stir in cheese.

- Place pumpkin in a heat-proof serving dish. Spoon mixture into pumpkin.

- Pour in enough chicken broth to come within ½" of the rim.

- Lay bay leaf on top and replace cover.

- Bake for 1½ hours or until pumpkin begins to soften on the outside and the contents begin to bubble.

- Reduce heat to 350°F. and bake ½ hour more until tender.

- Just before serving, stir in cream and parsley.

- Scoop some flesh from sides of pumpkin into each serving.

6 – 8 SERVINGS

Squash Apple Bisque

A pairing of traditional New England ingredients, apples and squash. The result is delicate, different and so delicious.

4 cups chicken stock

1 medium butternut squash, seeded, peeled and chopped

2 large McIntosh apples, peeled, cored and chopped

1 small onion, peeled and chopped

Pinch of rosemary

3 tablespoons unsalted butter

3 tablespoons flour

½ cup heavy or light cream

Salt and freshly ground black pepper, to taste

GARNISH:

Chopped, dried apples

- In large saucepan, combine stock, squash, apples, onion and rosemary over low heat. Cover and simmer until squash is tender, 10 – 15 minutes.

- Purée in blender or food processor. Set mixture aside in large bowl.

- In same saucepan, melt butter, stir in flour all at once and cook for 1 – 2 minutes over medium heat, stirring.

- Stir in squash purée. Simmer uncovered, 10 minutes over low heat.

- Add cream and season to taste with salt and pepper.

- Serve garnished with dried apples.

6 – 8 SERVINGS

Note: Recipe can be made without cream.

Baked Fish Chowder

2 pounds firm, boneless fish fillets, cut into large pieces

4 potatoes, peeled, sliced thin

3 onions, sliced thin

3 celery tops, chopped

1 bay leaf

4 whole cloves

1 garlic clove, minced

¼ teaspoon dill

¼ teaspoon freshly ground black pepper

2 teaspoons salt

5⅔ tablespoons butter

½ cup dry white wine

2 cups boiling water

2 cups light cream

GARNISH:

Chopped parsley

- Preheat oven to 375°F.

- In 4-quart heat-proof dish, place fish, potatoes, onions, celery, bay leaf, cloves, garlic, dill, pepper, salt, butter, wine and water.

- Cover and bake for 1 hour.

- Remove from oven. Add cream to chowder and stir well.

- Serve garnished with parsley.

8 – 10 SERVINGS

Note: *Best done one day in advance. Use any firm boneless fish fillets, like haddock, scrod, flounder, snapper or experiment with a combination of fish pieces.*

Corn Stew

Sweet corn is a local Massachusetts crop.

½ cup minced salt pork

2 tablespoons chopped onion

1 tablespoon chopped leek

½ cup chopped celery

3 tablespoons chopped green pepper

1 cup chopped potato, peeled

2 cups water

½ teaspoon salt

¼ teaspoon white pepper

½ bay leaf

¼ teaspoon marjoram

3 tablespoons all purpose flour

½ cup milk

1½ cups light cream or half and half, hot

2 cups fresh corn cut from the ear or frozen

GARNISH:

Chopped parsley

- In a heavy saucepan sauté the salt pork until lightly browned. Add the onion, leek, celery, and pepper and cook until golden brown.

- Add potato, water, salt, bay leaf and marjoram and simmer about 45 minutes until potato is tender.

- Bring to a boil and add flour and milk. Stir well.

- Add hot cream and corn. Reduce heat. Do not boil soup. Simmer for 10 minutes. Serve immediately garnished with parsley.

6 SERVINGS

Granary Burying Ground

Just off Tremont Street, next to the Park Street Church, is the third oldest cemetery in Boston. Established in 1660, the Granary Burying Ground stands near land once used for the town's granary and workhouse. Here are buried many illustrious early Bostonians including John Hancock, Samuel Adams and Robert Treat Paine (three signers of the Declaration of Independence), Paul Revere, eight former governors, Ben Franklin's parents, the victims of the famous Boston Massacre and many other patriots and colonists.

Indian Summer Cold Curry Apple Soup

This very unusual velvety smooth cold soup is so aromatic and tasty that you will want to serve it all year.

The Boston Marathon is run on a holiday unique to Massachusetts, Patriot's Day, the third Monday in April.

4 tablespoons unsalted butter

1 medium onion, sliced

3 medium McIntosh or Cortland apples, pared, cored and chopped

1 carrot, chopped

1 green pepper, chopped

1 stalk celery, chopped

Pinch of ground cloves

1 – 2 teaspoons curry powder

1 parsley sprig, minced

Pinch of freshly grated nutmeg

6 cups chicken stock

Salt and freshly ground black pepper, to taste

2 cups whipping cream, divided (1 cup room temperature, 1 cup chilled)

GARNISH:

1 apple, chopped

- In heavy 4-quart saucepan, melt butter.
- Add onion and sauté until soft and translucent.
- Add apples, carrot, green pepper and celery and sauté until soft and wilted.
- Stir in cloves, curry powder, parsley and nutmeg.
- Add chicken stock.
- Season to taste with salt and pepper.
- Simmer for 30 to 40 minutes. Remove from heat, let cool 2 minutes.
- Blend in 1 cup of room temperature whipping cream.
- Transfer to blender, and purée in batches until smooth.
- Cover and refrigerate. Ladle into chilled bowls when ready to serve.
- Whip remaining cream.
- Garnish each serving with a dollop of cream and chopped apple.

6 – 8 SERVINGS

Note: This may be prepared 2 to 3 days in advance without adding the cream. May be prepared fully, 1 day ahead. Do not chop apple for garnish until just before serving.

Granary Burying Ground

King's Chapel

Chilled Tomato Soup

2 tablespoons vegetable oil

2 cups chopped onions

¾ cup chopped carrots

1 tablespoon minced garlic

¼ teaspoon cayenne pepper

4 cups chicken stock

4 pounds plum tomatoes, peeled, seeded and chopped

2 tablespoons tomato paste

¼ cup fresh basil leaves

A very simple and quick summer soup.

Serve with fresh garlic croutons.

GARNISH:

1 – 2 green onions, finely chopped

- Heat oil in heavy 4 – 5 quart saucepan over medium heat.
- Add onions, carrots and garlic and cook until vegetables are softened, stirring occasionally, about 15 minutes.
- Mix in pepper. Add stock and simmer 30 minutes.
- Increase heat to high. Add tomatoes and tomato paste and cook until softened, about 10 minutes.
- Add basil. Purée soup in food processor or blender. Transfer to bowl, cover and chill.
- Ladle into chilled bowls when ready to serve. Garnish with green onions.

6 SERVINGS

Note: Can be prepared up to one day ahead.

Chilled Raspberry Soup

Icy and refreshing. This soup is a delightful Indian summer treat.

The winner of the Boston Marathon receives a laurel wreath, $45,000 and a new Mercedes Benz.

1 quart fresh ripe raspberries, rinsed and dried

1 tablespoon grated fresh ginger root

2 cups ginger ale

¼ cup raspberry liqueur

1 tablespoon chopped fresh mint leaves

¼ teaspoon freshly grated nutmeg

¼ teaspoon ground cinnamon

Pinch of salt

GARNISH:

4 tablespoons sour cream

4 fresh mint leaves

- In a food processor or blender, purée raspberries, ginger root, ginger ale, raspberry liqueur, mint, nutmeg, cinnamon and salt.

- Force the mixture through a sieve. Chill overnight.

- Ladle into chilled bowls when ready to serve. Garnish with sour cream and a fresh mint leaf.

4 SERVINGS

Note: Strawberries work equally well, in place of raspberries.

Cream of Cucumber Soup

4 large cucumbers

½ cup minced green onions

3 tablespoons butter

6 cups chicken stock

¾ teaspoon dill

4 tablespoons farina

Salt and freshly ground black pepper, to taste

1½ tablespoons tarragon vinegar, or to taste

1 cup light cream, sour cream or crème fraîche

GARNISH:

Thinly sliced cucumber

Minced dill or parsley

- Peel the cucumbers, slice in half lengthwise, scoop out and discard the seeds. Slice thinly and reserve.

- Cook the onion in butter slowly until tender but not browned.

- Add the cucumbers. Stir and cook for 1 – 2 minutes.

- Add the broth and dill. Bring to a boil.

- Stir in the farina and simmer mixture for 20 – 25 minutes.

- Purée mixture in a blender or food processor.

- Return to pan and season with salt and pepper. Add tarragon vinegar to taste.

- Let soup cool, then add cream. Cover and chill.

- Taste carefully for seasoning, as most cold soups require more salt.

- Ladle into chilled bowls when ready to serve.

- Garnish with cucumber slices and minced dill or parsley.

6 SERVINGS

Note: Soup may be prepared in advance. It may also be served hot.

How long is the Boston Marathon route? From Hopkinton to Boston, it is 26 miles, 385 yards.

Chilled Fruit Soup

This refreshing and unusual soup is perfect for a hot summer night.

2 pints strawberries

½ cup granulated sugar

½ cup water

Leaves from 3 sprigs fresh mint

¼ ripe cantaloupe

¼ cup fresh lemon juice

¼ cup fresh lime juice

Maple syrup, to taste

GARNISH:

Crème fraîche

Mint leaves

- Wash and hull strawberries.

- Place berries in food processor and purée.

- Boil together sugar and water until sugar is completely dissolved.

- Add mint leaves to sugar water syrup and steep until mixture is cooled, approximately 1 hour.

- Remove and discard mint leaves.

- Add sugar water syrup, cantaloupe, lemon and lime juices and maple syrup to strawberries in food processor.

- Purée the mixture and strain through sieve.

- Chill well before serving.

- Ladle into chilled bowls when ready to serve.

- Garnish with crème fraîche and fresh mint leaves.

8 SERVINGS

Carrot Vichyssoise

1 tablespoon butter

2 bunches green onions, chopped

2 cups chicken broth, divided

2 cups cooked carrots

½ teaspoon salt

⅛ teaspoon freshly ground black pepper

1 cup milk

GARNISH:

1 tablespoon chopped chives

- In a small saucepan, melt butter. Add green onions and cook over medium heat 5 minutes.

- Add 1 cup chicken broth to onions and cook covered, for 15 minutes.

- Pour all the chicken broth with onion, reserved chicken broth, carrots, salt and pepper into a blender or food processor.

- Blend mixture until smooth, approximately 1 minute.

- Add 1 cup milk. Transfer to bowl, cover and chill.

- Ladle into chilled bowls when ready to serve.

- Garnish with chives.

4 SERVINGS

Note: *This colorful cold vichyssoise needs a day of chilling to develop its flavor.*

Drizzle Parsley Cream through the soup in a decorative pattern for pizazz.

Parsley Cream

½ cup heavy cream
¼ cup parsley, minced

Place cream and parsley in processor. Process until smooth and very green. Refrigerate until ready to serve.

Fresh Pea Soup

3 tablespoons unsalted butter

1 medium onion, coarsely chopped

2 cups chicken broth

1 potato (approximately ¼ pound) peeled and coarsely chopped

3 cups fresh peas or frozen tiny peas

3 tablespoons minced fresh parsley

1 teaspoon chervil

3 tablespoons minced fresh or 1 teaspoon dried mint

2 cup water

½ teaspoon white pepper

GARNISH:

⅓ cup plain yogurt or crème fraîche

- In a heavy saucepan melt butter over medium heat.
- Add onion and cook until translucent.
- Add chicken broth and potato and bring to a boil.
- Reduce heat, cover and simmer 12 minutes until potato is tender.
- Add peas and simmer until peas are just tender, approximately 6 minutes.
- Add parsley, chervil and mint. Remove from heat.
- Purée soup in food processor or blender in batches.
- Pour soup into a heavy saucepan and add water and pepper. Heat through.
- Chill soup. Serve garnished with a swirl of yogurt.

4 SERVINGS

Note: This soup can also be served warm.

SALADS

King's Chapel

At the corner of Tremont and School Streets stands Boston's first Anglican house of worship, King's Chapel. Founded in 1688 by the Royal Governor, the Chapel has gone through many transformations from a small wooden structure for British officers to a grand Unitarian church made of Quincy granite. It wasn't until 1748 that the congregation raised adequate funds to enlist the services of the architect Peter Harrison of Newport, Rhode Island. His design called for a stone building, tower and wooden steeple. The cornerstone was laid in 1749 and construction proceeded around the old wooden Chapel. By 1753, the inner original Chapel was torn down and literally "thrown out the windows" of the new granite church. King's Chapel continued to undergo change until 1800.

Today, regular services are conducted for the First Unitarian congregation. Next door is the Chapel's burying ground, Boston's first cemetery and final resting place for nearly all of Boston's early settlers including the famous first governor, John Winthrop. Originally the vegetable garden of a Puritan, the site became the Bay Colony's burying ground in 1631. Also buried here are Mary Chilton, the first Pilgrim to step foot off the Mayflower at Plymouth and William Dawes, the lesser known midnight rider who, with Paul Revere in 1775, warned the sleeping colonists that the British were on the way.

Pecan Salad with Raspberry Vinaigrette

A delicious and colorful salad that can stand alone.

The pecans add crunch to this zesty salad.

SALAD:

2 heads Bibb lettuce, well washed

1 cup pecan halves, roasted and salted

½ cup blue cheese, crumbled

4 small red onions, thinly sliced

DRESSING:

2 cups vegetable oil

⅔ cup red wine vinegar

⅓ cup seedless raspberry jam

1 teaspoon dill

½ teaspoon dry mustard

¼ teaspoon white pepper

½ teaspoon salt

2 tablespoons granulated sugar

- TO PREPARE THE SALAD: Combine together in large salad bowl the lettuce, nuts, cheese and onions.
- TO PREPARE THE DRESSING: Mix together the oil, vinegar, jam, dill, mustard, pepper, salt and sugar. Blend well.
- Pour dressing on salad and toss gently. Serve immediately.

6 SERVINGS

Bacon Cheese Broccoli Salad

SALAD:

1 bunch broccoli, cut into small flowerets

½ pound bacon, cooked and crumbled

½ pound Cheddar cheese, grated

1 medium red onion, thinly sliced (approximately 1 cup)

DRESSING:

1 cup mayonnaise

½ cup granulated sugar

2 tablespoons red wine vinegar

- TO PREPARE THE SALAD: Cook the broccoli uncovered until tender-crisp. Drain well.

- Combine broccoli, bacon, cheese and onion in bowl.

- TO PREPARE THE DRESSING: Whisk together mayonnaise, sugar and vinegar.

- Pour dressing on salad, coating very lightly, and toss gently. Serve immediately.

6 – 8 SERVINGS

Combine orange and white Cheddar cheese for visual interest. A sweet and sour vegetable salad that is a meal in itself.

Chicken and Dill Salad

This salad is spectacular despite its simplicity.

Chicken may be poached in canned chicken broth for added flavor.

Add ⅔ cup julienned red and yellow pepper for added crunch and color.

6 whole chicken breasts

1 large bunch fresh dill, minced

6 green onions, diced

3 tablespoons capers

⅔ cup chopped red, yellow or green peppers (optional)

½ cup red onion, thinly sliced (optional)

DRESSING:

1 egg yolk

⅓ cup red wine vinegar

1 tablespoon minced garlic

2 teaspoons granulated sugar

Salt and freshly ground black pepper, to taste

1 cup olive oil

GARNISH:

Lettuce leaves or watercress sprigs

12 cherry tomatoes, halved

- Cook chicken breasts in boiling water until just cooked.

- Cool, remove skin and discard. Pull meat away from bones in largest possible chunks and cut in long, julienne slices.

- Mix chicken with dill, green onions, capers, peppers and red onion.

- TO PREPARE THE DRESSING: Combine egg yolk, vinegar, garlic, sugar, salt and pepper in food processor with metal blade. While motor is running, slowly add olive oil until dressing is creamy.

- Pour dressing on salad and toss gently.

- Arrange chicken slices on platter of lettuce or watercress and garnish with cherry tomato halves.

8 SERVINGS

Gorgonzola Tomato Salad

¼ **pound Gorgonzola cheese**

6 tomatoes

¼ **cup minced fresh parsley**

3 tablespoons sliced shallots

2 tablespoons minced fresh basil (or 2 teaspoons dried)

2 teaspoons Dijon mustard

2 tablespoons fresh lemon juice

⅓ **cup olive oil**

Salt and freshly ground black pepper, to taste

- Freeze the Gorgonzola for 30 minutes or until it is firm enough to grate.

- Slice the tomatoes thinly and arrange them overlapping in a circle on a large platter.

- Grate the Gorgonzola into a bowl.

- Add the minced parsley, shallots and basil.

- Sprinkle the mixture over the tomatoes.

- TO PREPARE THE DRESSING: Combine the mustard and lemon juice. Whisk in the olive oil and season with salt and pepper.

- Pour the dressing over the tomatoes.

6 SERVINGS

Very easy and tasty.

A great variation on the traditional sliced tomato salad.

Boston Potato Salad

Choose a potato low in starch when making potato salad. It will keep its shape and stay intact. To test for the starchiness of a potato, rub together cut potato halves. The starch will appear as a white froth.

5 large potatoes or 15 small red skinned potatoes (1 – 1½ pounds)

5 tablespoons red wine vinegar, divided

⅓ cup mayonnaise

⅓ cup sour cream

¼ cup finely chopped red onion

4 green onions, green part only, finely chopped

Salt to taste

1 tablespoon freshly ground black pepper

6 pieces of bacon cooked until very crisp

- Boil unpeeled potatoes in large saucepan with salted water until potatoes are just tender.
- Drain potatoes and peel while hot (red skins may be left on).
- Slice potatoes into ½" thick pieces.
- Toss warm potatoes with ¼ cup vinegar.
- Cool potatoes completely.
- Whisk together mayonnaise, sour cream and 1 tablespoon vinegar.
- Toss cooled potatoes with red and green onions, salt and pepper.
- Pour dressing over potatoes stirring gently.
- Crumble bacon over salad and stir gently.
- Refrigerate at least one hour, or overnight, before serving.

6 – 8 SERVINGS

Roasted Red Pepper Salad

6 large sweet red peppers

5 large tomatoes

20 black olives, pitted and quartered

¼ cup olive oil

1 teaspoon cumin

4 garlic cloves, crushed

1 tablespoon chopped parsley

Salt and freshly ground black pepper, to taste

- Preheat broiler. Broil peppers whole, until blistered.
- Put peppers in brown paper bag to sweat.
- When cool, remove skins, stem and seeds.
- Rinse quickly and dry on paper towels.
- Cut into strips.
- Cut tomatoes in half, through the stem ends.
- Squeeze out seeds or use a small spoon to scrape out seeds.
- Drain, cut side down, on paper towels.
- Cut into strips similar in size to peppers.
- TO PREPARE THE DRESSING: In a small bowl, combine olives, olive oil, cumin, garlic and parsley. Stir well.
- Combine dressing with pepper and tomato strips, mixing well.
- Season with salt and pepper.
- Refrigerate 3 hours before serving.

8 SERVINGS

A garlic lovers dream. Serve with PORK TENDERLOIN GRILL for a summer barbecue.

Warm Oriental Broccoli, Cauliflower and Pepper Salad

To toast sesame seeds, sprinkle on a baking sheet and lightly brown in a moderate oven (350°F.) or toaster oven. Shake or stir occasionally.

1 head broccoli, cut into flowerets

1 head cauliflower, cut into flowerets

2 red and/or yellow peppers, sliced thin

1 tablespoon freshly grated ginger root

2 garlic cloves, minced

2 tablespoons sesame oil

4 tablespoons peanut oil

2 tablespoons sherry vinegar

1 tablespoon sherry

2 teaspoons soy sauce

2 teaspoons fresh lemon juice

GARNISH:

½ cup sesame seeds, toasted

- TO PREPARE THE SALAD: Blanch broccoli and cauliflower for 3 – 4 minutes in boiling water. Remove and plunge into cold water.

- Blanch peppers for 1 minute in boiling water. Remove and plunge into cold water.

- Pat vegetables dry. Keep them at room temperature.

- TO PREPARE THE DRESSING: In food processor or blender, combine ginger, garlic, sesame oil, peanut oil, vinegar, sherry, soy sauce and lemon juice. Blend until creamy.

- Heat dressing until hot, being careful not to boil.

- Pour dressing on vegetables and toss gently. Garnish with sesame seeds.

6 – 10 SERVINGS

Note: *The ginger flavor is subtle. Do not substitute powdered ginger for freshly grated ginger root.*

Three Lettuce Salad with Dijon Vinaigrette

SALAD:

1 head Radicchio

1 head Romaine

1 head Boston lettuce

½ pound mushrooms

½ English cucumber

DIJON VINAIGRETTE:

1 tablespoon Dijon mustard

3 tablespoons red wine vinegar

1 teaspoon granulated sugar

½ teaspoon salt

½ teaspoon freshly ground black pepper

½ cup olive oil

½ cup safflower oil

- Wash cucumber. Slice thinly, and crisp slices in cold water in refrigerator for 2 hours. Drain.

- Wash and dry Radicchio, Romaine and Boston lettuce and tear into bite-size pieces.

- Clean mushrooms and slice.

- TO PREPARE VINAIGRETTE: Whisk together mustard, vinegar, sugar, salt and pepper.

- Slowly whisk in oils.

- Toss together lettuces, mushrooms and cucumber with vinaigrette.

- Serve immediately.

4 – 6 SERVINGS

Radicchio adds color and tang to this versatile salad.

Blue Cheese Medley Salad

A hearty salad that can stand alone as a meal.

SALAD:

2 cups fresh spinach

2 cups red leaf lettuce

2 cups Romaine

2 cups Boston lettuce

2 – 3 cups chopped ham

1 cup shredded carrots

½ cup chopped green pepper

DRESSING:

1 package (8 ounces) cream cheese, softened

3 ounces blue cheese, crumbled

½ cup plus 2 tablespoons milk

¼ cup mayonnaise

1 tablespoon chopped fresh chives

2 teaspoons fresh lemon juice

GARNISH:

1 cup croutons

- TO PREPARE THE SALAD: Place half of each of the following ingredients in the order listed in a large glass bowl: spinach, red leaf, Romaine, Boston lettuce, ham, carrots and green pepper.

- TO PREPARE THE DRESSING: In a small bowl, combine cream cheese with blue cheese until blended.

- In a medium bowl, combine milk, mayonnaise, chives and lemon juice. Add cheese mixture, mix well.

- Spread half of the dressing on salad.

- Repeat layering the remaining salad ingredients as above. Top salad with the remaining dressing.

- Cover the salad tightly and chill.

- Just before serving sprinkle salad with croutons.

8 – 10 SERVINGS

Note: This salad should be made only a few hours before serving.

Condiment Curried Chicken Salad

2 cups chicken broth

4 pounds chicken breasts, boned and split

1 can (8 ounces) water chestnuts, drained and sliced

2 pounds seedless grapes

2 – 3 cups sliced celery

2¼ cups mayonnaise

4½ teaspoons soy sauce

4½ teaspoons fresh lemon juice

2¼ teaspoons curry powder

1 cup sliced almonds

Lettuce leaves

- In large skillet, bring chicken broth to a boil.
- Add halved chicken breasts, adding water to cover if needed.
- Reduce heat to simmer. Cover and simmer for 15 minutes or until firm to touch.
- Turn off heat, let chicken cool in broth with cover ajar.
- Drain chicken. Cut into bite-size chunks.
- Mix together water chestnuts, grapes, celery, mayonnaise, soy sauce, lemon juice, curry powder and almonds.
- Add mixture to chicken. Toss well to blend.
- Cover and chill for several hours.
- Serve on bed of lettuce.

8 – 10 SERVINGS

Note: Salad must be made in advance. Keeps well covered in refrigerator. Can be halved, doubled or tripled.

An interesting variation on the standard chicken salad. Serve in scooped out papaya and garnish with red blush grapes.

A wonderful combination of texture, flavors and colors. This salad is best made in the fall when apples and beets are at their peak.

... sh lemon juice

½ teaspoon salt

½ cup vegetable oil

Freshly ground black pepper, to taste

½ head Romaine

2 Granny Smith or other firm, tart apples (peeled, cored and cut into ½″ cubes)

1 cup crumbled Roquefort cheese

½ cup chopped walnuts

⅓ cup minced green onions

- TO PREPARE THE BEETS: Place raw beets in medium saucepan filled with cold water.

- Bring to boil, reduce heat and simmer 15 – 45 minutes until beets are tender and can be pierced with a fork.

- Drain beets and cool slightly to peel.

- To peel beets, run them under cold water to slip skins off. Keep beets warm.

- TO PREPARE THE DRESSING: Combine lemon juice, salt, vegetable oil and pepper while beating in a small bowl.

- In another bowl, toss the warm beets with half the dressing and let stand for at least 30 minutes.

- Tear the Romaine into bite-size pieces.

- In a small bowl, mix the Romaine with apples, cheese, walnuts and onions.

- Gently toss the salad and use the remaining dressing as needed.

4 SERVINGS

Site of First Public School and Franklin Statue

The first public school in the United States stood at what is now Old City Hall on School Street. Known as the Boston Latin School, it was established in 1636 to provide the best in classical education for young colonists, many of whom went on to continue their education at Harvard College in Cambridge. Famous former students include Cotton Mather, John Hancock and Samuel Adams.

Another famous graduate of the Boston Latin School was Benjamin Franklin whose bronze statue is prominently situated in front of Old City Hall. One of the most famous early Americans, this Bostonian was an inventor, printer, editor, military officer, politician, statesman and signer of the Declaration of Independence. He is remembered also for establishing an academy in 1751 that developed into the University of Pennsylvania, inventing the Franklin stove and publishing *Poor Richard's Almanack*. Franklin also worked tirelessly for the cause of peace in the 1760's and 1770's both here and in Europe. He died in Philadelphia in 1790, and although his body is interred in Paris, Franklin is very much considered Boston's own.

Apple-Molasses Bread

Molasses is 100 percent natural. It is pure and contains no artificial additives.

It has more nutritional value than any other sweetener, including honey, maple syrup or sugar.

Molasses contains the minerals phosphorous and calcium.

1 stick butter or margarine

1 cup granulated sugar

3 eggs

2 cups all purpose flour

1½ teaspoons baking powder

1 teaspoon ground cinnamon

½ teaspoon freshly grated nutmeg

½ teaspoon ground cloves

1 cup applesauce

¼ cup molasses

1 cup raisins (optional)

½ cup chopped nuts (optional)

- Preheat oven to 350° F. Grease and flour a 9″ × 5″ × 3″ loaf pan.

- In a large bowl, cream butter and sugar.

- Add eggs, beating well after each addition.

- Sift together flour, baking powder, cinnamon, nutmeg and cloves.

- Combine applesauce with molasses.

- Add applesauce mixture to egg mixture.

- Add flour mixture to wet ingredients, stirring to mix well.

- Fold in raisins and nuts.

- Pour batter into prepared pan.

- Bake 50 – 60 minutes until cake tester inserted comes out clean.

1 LOAF

Date Nut Bread

1 package (8 ounces) pitted
   dates

1 cup boiling water

1 tablespoon butter or
   margarine

¾ cup granulated sugar

1½ cups all purpose flour

1 teaspoon baking soda

1 egg

1 teaspoon vanilla extract

½ teaspoon ground
   cinnamon

⅛ teaspoon freshly grated
   nutmeg

¼ teaspoon mace

½ teaspoon salt

1 cup chopped walnuts

- Preheat oven to 300°F. Grease a 9″ × 5″ × 3″ loaf pan.
- Cut dates into small pieces. Combine dates with boiling water, butter and sugar. Let stand until cool.
- Add flour, baking soda, egg, vanilla, cinnamon, nutmeg, mace, salt and walnuts. Stir until thoroughly mixed.
- Pour batter into prepared pan. Bake 1 hour. Cool thoroughly before slicing,

1 LOAF

Note: Freezes well.

Beacon Hill Banana Bread

2 cups all purpose flour

1 teaspoon baking soda

½ teaspoon salt

½ cup vegetable shortening

1 cup granulated sugar

2 eggs slightly beaten

3 or 4 large, very ripe
   bananas, mashed

½ cup pecans (optional)

- Preheat oven to 325°F. Grease a 9″ × 5″ × 3″ loaf pan.
- Mix flour, baking soda and salt together.
- In a large bowl, cream shortening and sugar.
- Blend dry ingredients with shortening mixture. Blend in eggs. Fold in bananas. Fold in pecans.
- Pour into prepared loaf pan. Bake for 45 – 60 minutes, until a cake tester inserted into center comes out clean.

1 LOAF

Note: Freezes well.

Fresh Autumn Pear Bread

Choose pears for baking which are still firm and not quite ripe enough to be eaten.

1 stick unsalted butter

1 cup granulated sugar

2 eggs, lightly beaten

1 teaspoon vanilla extract

2 cups all purpose flour

½ teaspoon salt

1 teaspoon baking powder

½ teaspoon baking soda

⅛ teaspoon freshly grated nutmeg

¼ cup buttermilk or yogurt

1 cup cored, coarsely chopped fresh ripe pears, skin left on

- Preheat oven to 350°F. Butter a 9″ × 5″ × 3″ loaf pan.

- With mixer, cream butter and sugar.

- Add eggs and vanilla.

- Combine flour, salt, baking powder, baking soda and nutmeg.

- Add flour mixture to butter mixture alternately with buttermilk, mixing gently but thoroughly.

- Gently stir in pears.

- Pour batter into prepared pan.

- Bake for 1 hour or until cake tester inserted into center comes out clean.

1 LOAF

Pilgrim Pumpkin Bread

1⅔ cup all purpose flour

1 teaspoon baking powder

¼ teaspoon salt

1 teaspoon baking soda

½ teaspoon ground cinnamon

½ teaspoon freshly grated nutmeg

½ teaspoon ground cloves

1½ cups granulated sugar

½ cup vegetable oil

2 eggs

1 cup canned pumpkin*

½ cup water

1 cup raisins or 1 cup chopped nuts or 1 cup pitted, chopped dates

- Preheat oven to 350°F. Grease a 9″ × 5″ × 3″ loaf pan.
- In a large bowl, combine the flour, baking powder, salt, baking soda, cinnamon, nutmeg, cloves and sugar.
- Add oil, eggs, pumpkin and water. Beat until smooth.
- Add one or more of raisins, dates or nuts and fold in.
- Pour batter into prepared pan. Bake for 1 hour.

1 LOAF

* If using fresh pumpkin, omit the water.

Botanically, pumpkins are a fruit and more precisely a berry. They are formed from the pistil of a single flower and are a member of the same family as cucumbers, gherkins and melons.

Zucchini Bread

3 eggs

1 cup vegetable oil

2 cups grated zucchini

2 cups all purpose flour

2 cups granulated sugar

1 teaspoon salt

1 teaspoon baking soda

1¼ teaspoons ground cinnamon

2 teaspoons vanilla extract

¾ teaspoon freshly grated nutmeg

1 teaspoon baking powder

- Preheat oven to 350°F. Grease and flour two 9″ × 5″ × 3″ loaf pans.
- In a large bowl, mix together eggs, oil, zucchini, flour, sugar, salt, baking soda, cinnamon, vanilla, nutmeg and baking powder.
- Divide mixture into two prepared pans. Bake for 1 hour or until a cake tester inserted into center comes out clean.

2 LOAVES

Note: Freezes well.

Small zucchini are preferred for eating as vegetables, but oversized ones do well in breads.

Buttermilk Cheese Cornbread

The addition of cream-style corn and cheese makes this a surprisingly moist and very flavorful cornbread.

1 cup yellow cornmeal

1 cup all purpose flour

1 tablespoon granulated sugar

1 teaspoon baking soda

½ teaspoon baking powder

¼ teaspoon salt

1 egg

¼ cup vegetable shortening, melted

¾ cup buttermilk

1 can (8 ounces) cream-style corn

½ cup grated Cheddar cheese

- Preheat oven to 425°F. Grease a 9" round or square pan and line with greased parchment or wax paper.

- In a large bowl, combine cornmeal, flour, sugar, baking soda, baking powder and salt.

- In another large bowl, whisk egg and shortening together.

- Add buttermilk and corn to egg mixture.

- Gently combine buttermilk mixture with flour mixture. Do not overmix.

- Gently fold cheese into batter. Do not overmix.

- Pour batter into prepared pan and bake for 35 minutes until firm and cake tester inserted into center comes out clean.

- Serve immediately.

8 SERVINGS

Tomato Herb Bread

1 package dry yeast

¼ cup warm water (105 – 115°F.)

6¼ teaspoons granulated sugar, divided

1½ cups milk

3 tablespoons butter, softened

2 teaspoons salt

7 – 9 cups all purpose flour

2 eggs, beaten

1 cup tomato, peeled, seeded and chopped

1 tablespoon dried onion

1 teaspoon basil

¼ teaspoon marjoram

¼ teaspoon thyme

To quickly peel tomatoes, drop into boiling water for 10 seconds for ripe tomatoes, 15 – 20 seconds for less mature ones.

- Dissolve yeast in warm water. Stir in ¼ teaspoon sugar. Let stand 10 minutes until bubbly.

- Heat milk and butter until warm.

- In a large bowl, mix salt, 6 teaspoons sugar and 2 cups flour. Add milk gradually, beating 50 strokes.

- Stir in yeast and ½ cup flour and beat 50 strokes.

- Mix in eggs, tomato, dried onion, basil, marjoram and thyme.

- Add enough flour to make soft dough.

- Turn dough onto lightly floured surface. Add flour to make workable.

- Knead until smooth and elastic about 10 minutes.

- Place dough in greased bowl, turn, cover and let rise until impression remains and double in size.

- Pound down and knead 3 minutes on floured board.

- Shape into desired loaf and place in 2 greased loaf pans. Let rise until double in size, about 45 minutes.

- Preheat oven to 350°F.

- Bake for 30 minutes.

2 LOAVES

Irish Soda Bread

One cup of buttermilk may be substituted in cooking with 1 tablespoon lemon juice or vinegar and enough regular milk to make 1 cup.

4 cups all purpose flour

1 cup granulated sugar

1 teaspoon baking soda

1 teaspoon salt

3 eggs

1½ cups buttermilk

1 – 2 teaspoons caraway seeds

1 cup raisins

- Preheat oven to 350°F. Prepare cast iron skillet by coating with vegetable oil and then flouring lightly.

- In a large bowl, mix flour, sugar, baking soda and salt.

- In a separate bowl, mix eggs and buttermilk.

- Add flour mixture to buttermilk mixture, mixing well.

- Stir in seeds and raisins.

- Pour mixture into skillet. Sprinkle with a tablespoon of sugar if desired.

- Bake for 45 – 60 minutes or until cake tester inserted into center comes out clean.

6 SERVINGS

Carrot Pineapple Bread

1 teaspoon baking soda

3 cups all purpose flour

1 teaspoon salt

2 cups granulated sugar

1½ teaspoons ground cinnamon

3 eggs, beaten

1 cup vegetable oil

1 cup crushed pineapple, drained

1 cup grated carrots

2 teaspoons vanilla extract

1 cup chopped nuts

- Preheat over to 325°F. Grease well two 9″ × 5″ × 3″ loaf pans.

- In a large bowl, sift together baking soda, flour, salt, sugar and cinnamon.

- Mix in eggs, oil, pineapple, carrots, vanilla and nuts.

- Pour into prepared pans. Bake 1 hour.

2 LOAVES

Boston Cheddar Cheese Bread

6 – 7 cups all purpose flour

1 tablespoon granulated sugar

1 tablespoon salt

2 tablespoons dry yeast

1½ cups water

¾ cup milk

3 cups shredded extra-sharp Cheddar cheese

- In large mixing bowl, combine 3 cups flour, sugar, salt and yeast.

- In a saucepan, combine water and milk and bring to just below boiling.

- Let cool.

- Blend milk mixture into dry ingredients beating and scraping the sides of bowl occasionally.

- Add cheese and an additional ½ cup flour.

- Turn out onto a floured surface and knead until smooth and elastic, working in only enough flour to control stickiness.

- Place in greased bowl, turning dough over to coat evenly.

- Cover and let rise in warm, draft-free place until doubled.

- Punch down and turn out onto floured surface and knead lightly.

- Cover and allow dough to rest 20 – 30 minutes.

- Punch down and divide in half.

- Shape into 2 loaves and place in greased 9″ × 5″ × 3″ loaf pans.

- Cover and let rise until doubled in bulk, about 45 – 60 minutes.

- Preheat oven to 375°F.

- Bake for 45 – 60 minutes or until bread makes a hollow sound when tapped on top.

- Cool on wire racks.

2 LOAVES

To convert measurements of shredded hard cheeses to pounds, a helpful rule of thumb is 4 cups equals 1 pound.

Weston Popovers with Apricot Butter

A popover recipe that never fails as long as you resist opening the oven door to peek.

Popovers:

3 eggs

1 cup milk

3 tablespoons butter, melted

1 cup all purpose flour

½ teaspoon salt

½ teaspoon ground ginger

Apricot Butter:

14 dried apricot halves

½ cup unsalted butter, cold and cut into pieces

Salt to taste

- Preheat oven to 375°F. Grease 4 custard or popover cups.
- TO PREPARE THE POPOVERS: In a large bowl, beat eggs, milk and butter.
- In another bowl, sift together the flour, salt and ginger.
- Beat the flour mixture into the egg batter until well mixed.
- Fill cups three quarters full.
- Bake 1 hour. Remove from oven. Serve immediately.
- TO PREPARE THE APRICOT BUTTER: In food processor, grind apricots to a paste. Add the butter and blend until smooth.
- Add salt to taste and transfer to serving bowl.
- Chill, covered.
- Remove from refrigerator 10 minutes before serving.

4 SERVINGS

Eventful Muffins

2¼ cups all purpose flour

1¼ cups granulated sugar

1 tablespoon ground cinnamon

2 teaspoons baking soda

½ teaspoon salt

½ cup pecans

½ cup shredded coconut

½ cup raisins

2 cups grated carrots

1 apple, shredded

1 can (8 ounces) crushed pineapple, drained

3 eggs

1 cup vegetable oil

1½ teaspoons vanilla extract

Healthful and delicious!

- Preheat oven to 350°F. Grease muffin tins or line with paper liners.

- Sift together flour, sugar, cinnamon, baking soda and salt.

- Combine flour mixture with pecans, coconut, raisins, carrots, apple and pineapple.

- In a separate bowl, whisk together the eggs, oil and vanilla.

- Combine mixtures and blend well.

- Spoon batter into muffin tins.

- Bake for 25 – 35 minutes.

- Cool in pan for 10 minutes after removing from oven. Remove from tins and finish cooling on rack.

24 MUFFINS

Note: These muffins need 24 hours to develop their full flavor. Freeze well.

Blueberry Sugar Tops

These are absolutely picture perfect muffins.

½ cup plus 2 tablespoons vegetable oil

1¼ cups granulated sugar

2 eggs

2 cups all purpose flour

2 teaspoons baking powder

½ teaspoon salt

½ cup milk

2 cups blueberries*

2 tablespoons all purpose flour

1 tablespoon granulated sugar

- Preheat oven to 375°F. Grease muffin tins, including top of pan.

- Beat together oil, 1¼ cups sugar and eggs.

- Add 2 cups flour, baking powder and salt alternately with milk.

- Mix blueberries with 2 tablespoons flour and add to batter.

- Divide batter evenly, piling to top of muffin cups.

- Sprinkle with sugar.

- Bake 25 – 30 minutes.

12 LARGE MUFFINS

* Fresh or frozen blueberries may be used.

Note: 2 cups chopped apples (unfloured) may be substituted for blueberries. Substitute cinnamon/sugar for sugar in this recipe.

Miniature Orange Muffins

2 sticks butter

1 cup granulated sugar

2 eggs

1 teaspoon baking soda

1 cup buttermilk

2 cups all purpose flour

Grated rind of 2 oranges, approximately 3 tablespoons

½ cup golden raisins or currants

- Preheat oven to 400°F. Butter well miniature muffin tins or line with paper liners.

- In a large bowl, cream together butter and sugar.

- Add eggs and beat until well mixed.

- Dissolve the baking soda in the buttermilk.

- Add buttermilk mixture alternately with the flour to the egg mixture.

- Add orange rind and raisins. Blend well.

- Fill prepared tins three-quarters full.

- Bake for 15 minutes.

- Remove muffins from tins immediately and keep warm on a serving plate.

48 MUFFINS

Cinnamon Sour Cream Cake

A perfect cake to have on hand in the freezer at holiday time.

Cake:

2 sticks butter, room temperature

1½ cups granulated sugar

4 eggs, room temperature

2 teaspoons vanilla extract

1 teaspoon almond extract

3 cups all purpose flour

2 teaspoons baking soda

3 teaspoons baking powder

½ teaspoon salt

2 cups sour cream

Topping:

1 cup chopped walnuts

⅓ cup granulated sugar

2 teaspoons ground cinnamon

- Preheat oven to 350°F. Grease a 10" bundt or tube pan or two 1½ quart round pans.

- TO PREPARE THE CAKE: Cream butter and sugar together until fluffy.

- Add eggs to butter mixture one at a time, beating well after each addition.

- Beat vanilla and almond extracts into butter mixture.

- Sift together flour, baking soda, baking powder and salt.

- Gradually add flour mixture to butter mixture.

- Gradually blend sour cream into batter.

- TO PREPARE THE TOPPING: Combine and stir together nuts, sugar and cinnamon.

- Pour half of cake batter into prepared pan(s).

- Sprinkle half of topping on batter.

- Spread remaining batter on topping. Cut with spatula, do not touch sides.

- Sprinkle with remaining half of topping.

- Bake for 60 – 75 minutes until cake tester inserted into center comes out clean.

8 – 10 SERVINGS

Note: *Baking time depends on size of pan(s) chosen. Cake tastes best after mellowing overnight. Freezes well.*

Benjamin Franklin Statue

The Globe Corner Bookstore

Blueberry Coffee Cake

Cake:

2 cups all purpose flour

1 cup granulated sugar

2 teaspoons baking powder

½ teaspoon salt

½ cup milk

1 stick margarine, melted

2 eggs

1 teaspoon vanilla extract

2 cups blueberries

Topping:

½ cup all purpose flour

½ cup granulated sugar

4 tablespoons butter, softened

1 teaspoon ground cinnamon

- Preheat oven to 350°F. Grease and flour an angel cake pan or 8″ × 10½″ pan.

- TO PREPARE THE CAKE: In a medium bowl, sift flour, sugar, baking powder and salt.

- In a large bowl, beat together milk, margarine, eggs and vanilla.

- Beat in flour mixture.

- Fold blueberries into batter and pour into prepared pan.

- TO PREPARE THE TOPPING: In a small bowl, combine flour, sugar, butter and cinnamon.

- Sprinkle topping on batter.

- Bake for 45 minutes until lightly browned and cake tester inserted into center comes out clean.

10 – 12 SERVINGS

Note: Freezes well.

Apple Muffin Cake

Try using a variety of apples when making this cake. McIntosh, Rome, Northern Spy and Golden Delicious all work well.

Cake:

⅓ cup fine plain bread crumbs

2 cups all purpose flour

1 tablespoon baking powder

1 teaspoon baking soda

1 teaspoon salt

1¼ teaspoons ground cinnamon

½ teaspoon allspice

¼ teaspoon ground cloves

1¼ cups granulated sugar

4 tablespoons butter

1 cup sour cream

2 eggs

1 cup peeled, finely diced apple

CRUMB TOPPING:

¼ cup granulated sugar

3 tablespoons all purpose flour

½ teaspoon ground cinnamon

2 tablespoons butter, cold

- Heat oven to 350°F. Grease 8 cup soufflé dish or 9″ tube pan. Sprinkle with bread crumbs, tapping out excess.

- TO PREPARE THE CAKE: Mix together flour, baking powder, baking soda, salt, cinnamon, allspice, cloves and sugar.

- Melt butter. Remove from heat and stir in sour cream. Beat in eggs.

- Combine butter mixture with flour mixture. Blend together 2 – 3 minutes.

- Stir in apple.

- Pour mixture in prepared pan.

- TO PREPARE THE TOPPING: Mix together sugar, flour, cinnamon and butter until it resembles coarse crumbs.

- Sprinkle topping on top of batter.

- Bake 45 – 60 minutes until a cake tester inserted in center comes out clean, if using soufflé dish. If using tube pan, test after 45 minutes.

- Cool thoroughly before removing from pan.

8 – 10 SERVINGS

Old Corner Bookstore

At the corner of School and Washington Streets is a quaint colonial brick building. Built in 1711 as an apothecary's shop, it is now a bookshop maintained by *The Boston Globe,* one of Boston's leading newspapers.

In 1828, the building was turned into a bookstore and from this point on it became a significant cornerstone in America's literary heritage. By 1833, it was in the hands of the famous publishing team of William Ticknor and James Fields. They gathered together many of the important literati of the time including Henry Wadsworth Longfellow, Harriet Beecher Stowe, Henry Thoreau, Oliver Wendell Holmes, Ralph Waldo Emerson, Nathaniel Hawthorne and Julia Ward Howe. The small bookstore soon became the regular meeting place of these noted authors. In 1857, it was here that America's oldest general interest magazine, *Atlantic Monthly,* was first launched.

The activities and patrons of the Old Corner Bookstore helped to earn nineteenth century Boston its reputation as "the Athens of America."

Dijon Rice and Shrimp Salad
in Pepper Cups

For a large gathering serve the rice and shrimp salad in a glass bowl. Chop the peppers and stir into rice mixture.

Peppers can be parboiled in a microwave oven.

1. Clean out and wash pepper, then dry.

2. Place pepper on a rack in the microwave.

3. Microwave on high for 1½ minutes (2 peppers at one time).

4 large peppers (green, red, yellow or purple), cored and seeded

2 tablespoons butter

2 tablespoons vegetable oil

½ cup finely chopped onion

⅓ cup peeled and finely chopped carrots

1 garlic clove, minced

½ cup medium raw shrimp, shelled and deveined and coarsely chopped

2½ cups warm cooked white rice

1 large tomato, seeded and chopped

½ cup Dijon mustard

1 tablespoon basil

½ cup freshly grated Parmesan cheese

Salt and freshly ground black pepper, to taste

- Parboil peppers in boiling salted water for 3 minutes. Drain and set aside.

- Heat butter and oil in a large deep pot.

- Add onions, carrots, garlic and sauté until slightly wilted.

- Add shrimp and cook until they are just firm and pink, about 3 minutes. Do not overcook.

- Add rice, tomato and mustard. Mix well.

- Remove mixture from heat.

- Add basil and cheese.

- Correct seasoning.

- Fill peppers with rice mixture.

- Serve warm or at room temperature.

4 SERVINGS

Ham and Spinach Soufflé Roll

SOUFFLÉ:

¼ cup butter

½ cup flour

½ teaspoon salt

⅛ teaspoon white pepper

2 cups milk

5 eggs, separated

FILLING:

2 tablespoons butter

4 shallots, finely chopped

4 medium mushrooms, chopped

1 cup cooked chopped spinach

1 cup cooked chopped ham

1 tablespoon Dijon mustard

¼ teaspoon freshly grated nutmeg

2 packages (3 ounces each) cream cheese, softened

Salt and freshly ground black pepper, to taste

- Preheat oven to 400°F. Grease and line a 10″ × 15″ jelly roll pan with wax paper. Grease again and dust with flour.

- TO PREPARE THE SOUFFLÉ: Melt butter in a saucepan. Blend in the flour, salt and pepper. Gradually stir in milk.

- Bring to a boil, stirring, and cook 1 minute.

- Beat the yolks, add a little hot sauce to yolks while beating.

- Add the yolk and sauce mixture to the pan and cook over medium heat 1 minute longer, stirring. Do not boil. Cool to room temperature.

- Beat the whites until stiff but not dry. Fold whites into cooled sauce. Spread in prepared pan.

- Bake for 25 – 30 minutes until well puffed and browned.

- TO PREPARE THE FILLING: While soufflé is baking, melt the butter in a skillet and sauté shallots until tender.

- Add the mushrooms and cook until they give up their moisture and it evaporates, about 3 minutes.

- Add spinach, ham, mustard and nutmeg and heat, stirring.

- Stir in cheese, salt and pepper.

- When soufflé is done, turn out onto a clean towel immediately and spread with filling. Roll, using tea towel to aid you.

- Slide onto serving platter with seam side down and serve warm.

6 SERVINGS

A festive and impressive entrée.

Makes a perfect centerpiece for a brunch buffet.

Asparagus and Chicken Crêpes

CRÊPES:

¾ cup flour

¾ cup milk

3 eggs

¼ cup water

½ teaspoon salt

3 tablespoons butter, clarified

FILLING:

1½ – 2 pounds asparagus (about 30 stalks), cut into ½" lengths

4 boneless chicken breasts, poached and diced

¼ cup fresh lemon juice

5 tablespoons butter, divided

¼ cup all purpose flour

1 cup chicken stock

1 cup heavy cream

½ cup freshly grated Gruyère cheese

6 tablespoons freshly grated Parmesan cheese, divided

1 egg yolk, lightly beaten

Salt and freshly ground black pepper, to taste

- TO PREPARE THE CRÊPES: In blender combine flour, milk, eggs, water and salt. Blend for 30 seconds scraping batter down from sides.

- Add 2 tablespoons cooled clarified butter and blend for a few more seconds.

- Transfer batter to a bowl. Let stand covered for at least 1 hour.

- Heat crêpe pan and brush lightly using remaining tablespoon of clarified butter. Repeat for each crêpe.

- Half fill a ¼ cup measure with batter and pour into crêpe pan for each crêpe.

- Cook crêpe over medium-high heat until lightly browned.

- Keep cooked crêpes on a plate covered with a dampened tea towel.

- Preheat oven to 400°F.

Continued on next page

- TO PREPARE THE FILLING: Cook asparagus and drain.

- In a large bowl, combine asparagus with diced chicken.

- Add lemon juice and salt and pepper to taste.

- Toss mixture to combine well.

- Cover mixture with a piece of buttered wax paper.

- In a heavy saucepan, melt 3 tablespoons of butter.

- Stir in flour and cook roux over low heat, stirring for 3 minutes.

- Remove pan from the heat.

- Heat chicken stock. Add to roux, stirring vigorously.

- Return roux to heat and simmer for 5 minutes, stirring occasionally.

- Stir in heavy cream and salt and pepper to taste.

- Combine ⅓ cup sauce with the chicken and asparagus mixture.

- Combine remaining sauce with Gruyère, 2 tablespoons Parmesan and egg yolk. Mix well.

- Divide chicken mixture among 8 crêpes. Roll to enclose filling.

- Arrange crêpes in baking pan in 1 layer. Pour sauce over them.

- Dot with 2 tablespoons of butter and remaining 4 tablespoons of grated Parmesan.

- Bake for 15 minutes, increase heat to broil and cook for 2 – 3 minutes until lightly brown.

8 SERVINGS

Note: *Crêpes may be easily prepared in advance and frozen. Place sheets of wax paper between the crêpes and wrap tightly in aluminum foil.*

Shrimp and Feta Salad

A delicious Greek seafood salad.

1 pound fusilli, or any medium to large spiral-shaped pasta

2 garlic cloves, minced

1 green pepper, diced

1 red pepper, diced

3 – 4 tablespoons olive oil

1 pound medium shrimp, cooked and deveined

10 – 12 ounces Feta cheese, crumbled

3 scallions with half of green part, diced

1 large or 2 medium tomatoes, diced

½ cup freshly grated Parmesan cheese

1 – 2 teaspoons oregano

3 tablespoons fresh parsley, minced

Salt and freshly ground black pepper, to taste

GARNISH:

Sprigs of fresh basil

- Cook pasta according to package instructions until al dente. Drain and place in a large bowl.

- Sauté garlic and green and red peppers in olive oil over medium heat for 3 – 5 minutes stirring constantly.

- Add shrimp and stir briefly. Remove from heat. Stir just until shrimp turn pink.

- Combine Feta, scallions, tomatoes, Parmesan, oregano and parsley with pasta. Add salt and pepper to taste.

- Combine shrimp mixture with pasta mixture, mixing well.

- Garnish with basil sprigs.

- Serve immediately at room temperature or chill before serving. If serving chilled, you may wish to add an additional 1 – 2 tablespoons of olive oil.

6 – 8 SERVINGS

Prosciutto Wrapped Hearts of Palm

1 can (14 ounces) hearts of palm, approximately 8 stalks

¼ pound thinly sliced Danish Fontina cheese

¼ pound thinly sliced Prosciutto

1 jar (7 ounces) roasted red peppers

- Preheat broiler.

- Rinse hearts of palm and remove any woody covering until all are uniform ¾″ diameter. Pat dry.

- Wrap stalks in Prosciutto, then in Fontina. Place in broiling pan.

- Lay strips of pepper across tops. Broil until cheese melts. Serve immediately.

4 SERVINGS

Note: Stalks of trimmed, steamed, thick asparagus could be substituted for the hearts of palm.

Choose only tender hearts of palm for this elegant and unique dish.

Swordfish with Greek Olives and Pasta

½ pound swordfish, 1″ thick

¾ cup chopped Greek olives

¼ cup irgin olive oil

½ cup thinly sliced onion

2 cloves garlic, minced

1 teaspoon oregano

1 tablespoon capers

½ pound pasta

- Preheat broiler and prepare broiling rack with foil.

- Broil swordfish for 3 minutes on the first side. Turn, top with olives and broil for 4 more minutes.

- In a sauté pan, cook onion and garlic in oil until soft. Add oregano and capers.

- Cook pasta until al dente and drain.

- Cut cooked swordfish into thin strips.

- In a large bowl, combine pasta, swordfish and onion-caper mixture gently. Serve immediately.

2 SERVINGS

Pasta, such as macaroni and spaghetti, will almost double in bulk when cooked while egg noodles will stay the same. One cup of uncooked rice will triple when steamed.

Smoked Salmon Soufflé

The timing of the various components of this recipe is the most difficult task. As with all recipes read the entire recipe thoroughly and organize each step and ingredient before you begin.

A wonderful rich brunch dish that is worth the extra effort.

6 tablespoons unsalted butter, divided

4½ tablespoons all purpose flour

1⅔ cup milk

2 anchovies, mashed, or 1 teaspoon anchovy paste

1 cup freshly grated Parmesan cheese, divided

4 egg yolks

¼ pound thinly sliced smoked salmon or lox, coarsely chopped

5 egg whites

Salt and freshly ground black pepper, to taste

- Preheat oven to 450°F.

- In a large saucepan, melt 4 tablespoons butter and add flour. Mix well with a wire whisk and cook, stirring frequently, for 3 – 5 minutes or until hot but not yet beginning to brown.

- Remove saucepan from heat and gradually whisk in milk until smooth.

- Return to medium heat and cook, stirring constantly, until mixture is very thick and begins to bubble when whisking stops.

- Lower the heat and cook for 5 minutes, stirring frequently.

- Remove from heat,

- Add anchovies to saucepan.

- Add pepper and ½ cup of Parmesan and stir until blended.

- Whisk in egg yolks.

- Return pan to stove and cook over medium heat, stirring constantly, until mixture thickens, 3 – 5 minutes. Do not let boil.

- Remove sauce from heat and stir in smoked salmon. Season with salt to taste.

- Generously grease 8″ soufflé dish with 2 tablespoons of butter. Add ¼ cup of Parmesan and tilt to coat dish thoroughly with cheese.

Continued on next page

- Beat egg whites until they hold stiff peaks. Fold ⅓ of the whites into the soufflé base, then gently fold this mixture into remaining egg whites until thoroughly mixed.

- Pour soufflé mixture into the prepared dish and sprinkle the top with the remaining ¼ cup of Parmesan.

- Bake for 5 minutes, lower heat to 350°F. and bake approximately 35 – 40 minutes until it has risen and is well browned on top.

- Gently remove soufflé from oven.

- Serve immediately.

10 SERVINGS

Note: *The soufflé base may be prepared one day in advance through addition of smoked salmon.*

Country Eggs

An unusual but very satisfying brunch entrée.

18 eggs, hard-cooked, thinly sliced

1 pound bacon, fried and crumbled

1 garlic clove, minced

4 tablespoons butter, melted

½ cup all purpose flour

1 cup whipping cream, room temperature

1 cup milk, room temperature

1 pound Chedddar cheese, grated

¼ teaspoon thyme

¼ teaspoon marjoram

¼ teaspoon basil

¼ cup minced fresh parsley

- Preheat oven to 350°F. Grease a 12-cup heat-proof dish.
- Sauté garlic in melted butter until transparent.
- Add flour, stirring constantly until mixture bubbles.
- Add cream and milk gradually while continually stirring.
- When mixture has thickened, add cheese, thyme, marjoram, basil and parsley and stir until cheese melts.
- Spoon ⅓ of sauce into prepared baking dish.
- Top with half of eggs and half of bacon.
- Spoon ⅓ more sauce on top and repeat egg and bacon layers.
- Top with remainder of sauce.
- Bake for 30 minutes.

10 – 12 SERVINGS

Note: *This works best if prepared 1 – 2 days in advance and refrigerated, then brought to room temperature before baking. Do not freeze. Recipe can easily be doubled.*

Zucchini and Tomato Torte

CRUST:

1 package saltine crackers, crushed, about 1 cup

¼ cup wheat germ

6 tablespoons butter, melted

A delightful way to serve summer squash.

FILLING:

1 large onion, sliced

1 zucchini squash, sliced

1 yellow summer squash, sliced

2 tablespoons butter

½ teaspoon salt

Freshly ground black pepper, to taste

¼ teaspoon marjoram

¼ teaspoon tarragon

1 cup grated Monterey Jack or Cheddar cheese

½ cup freshly grated Parmesan cheese

2 eggs

3 tablespoons milk

1 tomato, thinly sliced

- Preheat oven to 400°F.

- TO PREPARE THE CRUST: Combine saltines with wheat germ and melted butter.

- Press mixture on bottom and 1″ up on sides of 8″ springform pan.

- Bake for 8 – 10 minutes, until lightly browned. Reduce heat to 325°F.

- TO PREPARE THE FILLING: Sauté the onion and squashes in 2 tablespoons butter until crisp-tender. Drain off butter.

- In a bowl, mix sautéed vegetables with salt, pepper, marjoram and tarragon.

- Pour half the vegetable mixture into prepared crust and sprinkle with half the cheeses, then the remaining vegetables.

- Combine the eggs and milk and pour over the vegetables.

- Arrange the tomatoes over the top and sprinkle with the remainder of the cheeses.

- Bake for 45 – 50 minutes until torte is set.

4 SERVINGS

Leek and Ham Rolls

Serve with a tangy green salad and BUTTERMILK CORNBREAD. Could also be an elegant buffet dish.

4 tablespoons butter, divided

1 cup julienned leeks, white part only

2 tablespoons all purpose flour

½ cup milk, warmed

½ cup shredded Cheddar cheese

⅛ teaspoon white pepper

4 thin slices of ham

- Preheat broiler to medium. Lightly butter shallow heat-proof dish.

- In a small skillet, melt 2 tablespoons of butter. Sauté leeks in butter 2 – 3 minutes, making sure they are still firm.

- In small saucepan, melt remaining 2 tablespoons of butter and add flour to form roux. Cook 2 minutes, stirring.

- Slowly add warm milk to roux stirring until thick.

- Add cheese and pepper to cream sauce and stir until thick. Remove from heat.

- Divide leeks on the 4 slices of ham and roll up. Place rolls in prepared heat-proof dish.

- Pour cheese sauce over ham rolls.

- Place baking dish under broiler until rolls are bubbly and golden on top.

2 SERVINGS

Note: Can be doubled.

Pasta with Gorgonzola Sauce

1 shallot, minced

1 tablespoon unsalted butter

3 tablespoons dry vermouth

10 ounces crème fraîche

¼ pound imported Italian Gorgonzola

Freshly ground nutmeg, to taste

Freshly ground black pepper, to taste

¼ cup freshly grated Parmesan cheese

1 pound fettucine, cooked

- Sauté shallot in butter until transparent.

- Add vermouth and cook until almost evaporated.

- Add crème fraîche, mix and cook until slightly reduced.

- Add Gorgonzola, allowing to melt into sauce.

- Add nutmeg and pepper.

- Toss sauce with cooked pasta and serve sprinkled with Parmesan.

4 SERVINGS

A cheese lover's meal. Very rich and creamy. Serve over spinach or basil fettucine.

Bay Scallop Gougère

Nantucket Bay scallops are justifiably world famous. They are small, sweet, and succulent.

This gougère is extremely elegant and a unique scallop presentation.

GOUGÈRE DOUGH:

4 tablespoons butter

1 cup milk

1 cup all purpose flour

4 eggs

1 cup Gruyère or Italian Fontina, cut into ¼″ cubes

1½ teaspoons grainy mustard

½ teaspoon salt

½ teaspoon freshly ground black pepper

FILLING:

4 tablespoons butter

1½ pounds bay scallops

1 medium red onion, chopped

½ cup tarragon vinegar

1 cup heavy cream

1 tablespoon Dijon mustard

1 tablespoon grainy mustard

2 tablespoons medium-dry sherry

Salt and freshly ground black pepper, to taste

1 cup grated Gruyère or Italian Fontina

- Preheat oven to 400°F.

- TO PREPARE THE DOUGH: In a medium saucepan, heat the butter and milk to boiling. Remove from heat and add the flour all at once, stirring until the mixture is smooth and cleans the side of the pan.

- Put the dough in a food processor and add the eggs one at a time, processing well after each egg. Add the cheese, mustard, salt and pepper and process until smooth.

- Butter a 15″ × 10″ jelly roll pan. Spread the dough over the entire sheet, building up the sides and leaving just a thin layer of dough in the middle.

- Bake in middle of the oven until gougère is puffed and browned, approximately 30 minutes.

Continued on next page

- TO PREPARE THE SCALLOP FILLING: While the gougère is baking melt the butter in a large fry pan over medium-high heat. Add the scallops and sauté for one minute. Remove the scallops with a slotted spoon and set aside.

- Add the onion to the fry pan and sauté for 2 minutes.

- Pour in the vinegar and heat until just 1 tablespoon remains.

- Pour in the cream, then stir in the mustards and the sherry. Season with salt and pepper. Continue to cook until the mixture is very thick and reduced by about half. It will be the consistency of hollandaise. Remove from heat and stir in the scallops.

- When the gougère is puffed and evenly browned, spread the scallop mixture on top. Sprinkle with the grated cheese and return to the oven until the cheese is melted and browned, approximately 15 minutes. Do not overcook the scallops or they will become rubbery.

- Cut into squares and serve while hot.

10 – 12 SERVINGS

Confetti Shrimp Salad

A multicolored medley.

Serve in avocado halves garnished with wedges of hard boiled eggs.

SALAD:

2 cups fresh corn kernels, steamed 3 minutes (or substitute canned, drained corn)

½ red pepper, cut into thin strips

½ green pepper, cut into thin strips

36 medium or large shrimp, approximately 1 – 1½ pounds, cooked, peeled and deveined

MARINADE:

1 large egg yolk

¾ cup red wine vinegar

3 tablespoons Dijon mustard

¾ cup olive oil

¾ cup peanut oil

3 – 4 tablespoons chopped chives or 2 tablespoons dried

4 tablespoons minced fresh parsley

2 tablespoons minced shallots

GARNISH:

Small head Bibb lettuce, washed and separated into leaves

2 ripe tomatoes, cut into eighths

1 small red onion, thinly sliced

- TO PREPARE THE SALAD: Mix together corn and red and green peppers. Cover and refrigerate.

- TO PREPARE THE MARINADE: Mix together egg yolk, vinegar, mustard and oils until blended, approximately 1 minute with blender or processor. Add chives, parsley and shallots.

- Pour marinade over shrimp. Refrigerate 3 – 4 hours, stirring several times to enhance flavor.

- Before serving, mix shrimp with corn and peppers.

- Serve on a bed of lettuce, garnished with tomatoes and red onion.

6 SERVINGS

Brie Linguine

A very intense pasta that should be served as a side dish.

4 large, ripe tomatoes, peeled and coarsely chopped

1 small red onion, coarsely chopped

3 garlic cloves, finely minced

½ – ¾ cup fresh basil leaves, well washed and dried

½ cup olive oil

¾ pound Brie cheese, rind removed and broken into chunks

2 ounces Prosciutto, cut into thin strips

1 – 2 teaspoons salt

1 – 2 teaspoons freshly ground black pepper

4 sun-dried tomatoes, well-chopped (optional)

1 pound linguine

Garnish:

Freshly grated Parmesan cheese

- In a large bowl, mix together tomatoes, onion, garlic, basil, oil, Brie, Prosciutto, salt, pepper and sun-dried tomatoes.

- Cover and let sit at room temperature for at least 2 – 3 hours before serving.

- Cook linguine until al dente. Drain.

- Toss pasta with tomato mixture, correct seasoning and garnish generously with Parmesan.

6 SERVINGS SERVINGS

Note: Flavored fresh pasta such as red pepper, basil, spinach, etc. provides wonderful color and taste.

Tomato Sauce Alfresco

Very quick and easy.

Exceptional in the summer with the plumpest of red tomatoes.

Thin spaghetti or angel hair pasta are perfect for this light sauce.

½ cup olive oil

4 medium ripe tomatoes, peeled and finely chopped

1 garlic clove, minced

½ cup chopped fresh parsley

Pinch of salt

1 teaspoon chopped fresh basil

¼ teaspoon freshly ground black pepper

1 pound thin spaghetti

- In large bowl, combine oil, tomatoes, garlic, parsley, salt, basil and pepper.

- Let sauce sit at room temperature 1-2 hours prior to serving.

- Cook spaghetti al dente. Drain.

- Serve spaghetti in large bowl with sauce mixed in or as individual portions of spaghetti topped with sauce.

4 – 6 SERVINGS SERVINGS

Old South Meeting House

Across the street from the Old Corner Bookstore on Washington Street is the Old South Meeting House. Built in 1729 by Josiah Blanchard, the Old South Meeting House was used as a Congregational Church and, more importantly, as a place for large gatherings and town meetings. Grievances against the King and other matters were often discussed. Here in 1773, John Hancock gave the annual oration in memory of the Boston Massacre. One year earlier, Joseph Warren had given the same annual message, imploring "Our land be a land of Liberty, the seat of virtue, the asylum of the oppressed, a name and a praise in the whole earth."

The Old South Meeting House is synonymous with cause of American freedom. On December 16, 1773, Samual Adams and James Otis raised their voices to oppose the King's oppressive Stamp Act tariffs. More people than could be accommodated gathered at Faneuil Hall. The large crowd moved to the Old South Meeting House, Boston's largest building. The colonists had decided some weeks before that the tea recently arrived from England would be sent back unopened and without paying the King's tax. Incensed by Adams's speech, a group of men decided to destroy the tea that night. Paul Revere and Samual Adams were among the men that destroyed 342 chests of East India Company tea. This act of defiance is remembered as the Boston Tea Party. In retaliation, England closed the port of Boston. In May of 1774, British troops occupied the city and the patriots prepared to defend their homeland.

Florentine Chicken Breasts with Mustard Sauce

A very colorful and delicious way to serve poultry.

Serve with wild rice and BRAISED TARRAGON CHERRY TOMATOES.

CHICKEN:

½ pound Ricotta cheese

½ pound fresh spinach leaves

½ cup broccoli flowerets

Salt and freshly ground black pepper, to taste

Pinch of thyme

Pinch of tarragon

4 tablespoons butter

4 whole chicken breasts, boned but with skin left on

SAUCE:

¼ cup white wine

2 cups heavy cream

1 – 2 tablespoons Dijon mustard

- Preheat oven to 350°F.

- In food processor, add Ricotta, spinach, broccoli, salt, pepper, thyme and tarragon. Pulse a few times to chop.

- Using a sharp knife, lift the skin from the chicken to form a pocket, leaving three sides still attached.

- Stuff each breast with enough of the Ricotta-spinach mixture to form a compact pouch. Fold the sides of the breast underneath.

- Place the chicken breasts in a shallow roasting pan.

- Top each with a tablespoon of butter and bake for 1 hour or until the top is golden.

- TO PREPARE THE SAUCE: Remove chicken from roasting pan and move pan to top of stove. Keep chicken warm.

- Deglaze very hot pan with white wine, stirring.

- Add cream, stirring over medium-high heat, and add mustard to taste. Continue stirring until it thickens, about 10 minutes.

- Serve sauce over chicken breasts.

4 SERVINGS

Deviled Rock Cornish Hens

HENS:

4 Rock Cornish hens, about 1¼ pounds each, split along the backbone

Salt and freshly ground black pepper, to taste

¼ cup vegetable oil

4 tablespoons Dijon mustard

2 tablespoons dry white wine

¾ cup fine, fresh bread crumbs

DIABLE SAUCE:

1 tablespoon unsalted butter

2 tablespoons finely chopped shallots

¼ cup dry white wine

1 teaspoon Worcestershire sauce

½ cup chicken broth

1 tablespoon tomato paste

½ cup heavy cream

1 tablespoon very sharp imported mustard

Salt and freshly ground black pepper, to taste

- Preheat broiler to high.

- Place the split hens on a flat surface and pound lightly with a mallet to flatten.

- Sprinkle the hens with salt, pepper and oil on both sides.

- In a small bowl, combine the Dijon mustard and wine and set aside.

- Arrange the halves on a baking sheet skin side down and broil 3″ from heat 8 – 9 minutes. Turn halves over and continue to broil for 3 minutes.

- Turn oven to bake at 450°F.

- Brush both sides with mustard-wine mixture, turn skin side up and brush with pan drippings and sprinkle with bread crumbs. Return hens to oven for 15 minutes.

- TO PREPARE THE SAUCE: In a small saucepan, heat the butter and add the shallots. Cook briefly, stirring.

- Add the wine and reduce to 2 tablespoons.

- Add Worcestershire sauce and chicken broth, stir in tomato paste and reduce by almost half.

- Add cream, mustard, salt and pepper, and stir.

- Serve hens on top of a pool of Diable sauce.

4 SERVINGS

Mustard types are clearly defined and there are very distinct national styles.

American mustard is a bright yellow condiment made from the white mustard seed which is comparatively bland.

Dijon mustard is made from a darker variety of seed and is blended with white wine to make a sharper mustard.

Chutney Chicken Dijon

The chutney topping compliments the mustard marinated spiciness of the chicken.

2 whole chicken breasts, split, boned and skinned

½ cup Dijon mustard

½ cup all purpose flour

¼ cup shortening or vegetable oil

1 jar (10 ounces) Major Grey's chutney*

- In large mixing bowl, place chicken and mustard, coating chicken completely.
- Cover and let stand in refrigerator overnight.
- Preheat oven to 350°F.
- Dredge chicken in flour.
- In heavy skillet over medium heat, brown chicken on all sides in hot oil.
- Transfer chicken to 9″ × 13″ baking pan.
- Bake uncovered for 20 minutes or until chicken is tender.
- Remove chicken to serving platter.
- Liberally spoon chutney over chicken.

4 SERVINGS

* It is important to use Major Grey's chutney (made by several companies), as the mangoes add a distinctive flavor.

Note: *To cook in microwave, brown chicken as above, place in microwave dish, cover and cook on full power for 5 minutes. Top with chutney. Recipe can be prepared in advance and also frozen.*

Grape-Stuffed Rock Cornish Hens with Orange Butter

HENS:

2 Rock Cornish hens

2 tablespoons butter, room temperature

1 tablespoon finely grated orange peel

1 teaspoon minced fresh ginger root

1 teaspoon minced shallot

2 tablespoons butter, melted

1 tablespoon soy sauce

STUFFING:

2 tablespoons butter

¾ cup chopped onion

2 slices day-old white bread, crusts trimmed, cubed

2 tablespoons minced fresh parsley

½ teaspoon thyme

½ cup seedless red or black grapes

Salt and freshly ground black pepper, to taste

- Preheat oven to 425°F. Position rack in lower third of oven.

- TO PREPARE THE HENS: Make pocket in breast of each hen by carefully loosening skin with fingers.

- In a small bowl, combine 2 tablespoons butter with orange peel, ginger root and shallot and mix until smooth.

- Place half of butter mixture in each pocket and spread evenly by gently pressing down on skin with fingertips.

- TO PREPARE THE STUFFING: Melt 2 tablespoons butter in saucepan over low heat. Add onion and sauté until golden, about 7 minutes.

- Add bread, parsley and thyme and mix well.

- Blend in grapes. Taste and season with salt and pepper.

- Stuff hens with stuffing mixture and truss securely.

- In a small bowl, combine melted butter and soy sauce, brush over hens.

- Arrange hens on sides on rack in roasting pan. Roast 10 minutes. Turn hens to other side and roast 10 minutes more.

- Reduce oven temperature to 375°F. Turn hens, breast side up and continue roasting until hens are done, about 40 more minutes.

2 SERVINGS

Rock Cornish Game hens were created in America by cross breeding Cornish gamecocks and Plymouth Rock hens.

Orange Turkey Scaloppine

Turkey breast cutlets are a nice change from boneless chicken breasts.

This recipe is easy and elegant.

1 pound turkey breast cutlets, pounded ⅛" thick

All purpose flour for dredging

Salt and freshly ground black pepper, to taste

1 tablespoon vegetable oil

6 tablespoons butter, divided

½ cup freshly squeezed orange juice

½ cup white wine

1 tablespoon freshly grated or 1 teaspoon dried orange rind

1 teaspoon sage

¼ teaspoon thyme

GARNISH:

Minced fresh parsley

- Dredge the turkey in flour seasoned with salt and pepper. Shake off excess.

- Melt the oil and 4 tablespoons of the butter in large heavy skillet over high heat.

- Cook cutlets in skillet for 30 seconds on each side, transfer to warm plate and keep warm.

- Discard pan drippings.

- Add orange juice and wine to pan and scraping up browned bits, boil until glossy and reduced by ⅓, approximately 2 minutes.

- Add orange rind, sage and thyme to skillet and boil until sauce thickens and coats a spoon.

- Remove from heat and swirl in remaining 2 tablespoons butter.

- Pour any juices that have accumulated in turkey plate into pan and whisk into sauce.

- Arrange turkey on plates or platter and spoon sauce over turkey.

- Garnish with parsley.

4 SERVINGS

Chicken Piccata

2 boneless chicken breasts, split

½ cup all purpose flour

½ cup freshly grated Parmesan cheese

Salt and freshly ground black pepper, to taste

Garlic salt, to taste

Paprika, to taste

4 tablespoons butter

¼ cup white wine

3 tablespoons fresh lemon juice

GARNISH:

3 – 4 tablespoons capers

Lemon slices

- Pound chicken thin.

- Mix together the flour, cheese, salt, pepper, garlic salt and paprika.

- Dip chicken breasts in flour and cheese mixture.

- In skillet, melt butter over medium heat and cook chicken 3 – 4 minutes per side until chicken is no longer pink.

- Remove chicken to warm platter and drain pan.

- In same frying pan combine wine and lemon juice. Heat to boiling while stirring.

- Pour sauce over chicken.

- Garnish with capers and lemon slices.

4 SERVINGS

A very easy and quick method of preparing boneless chicken breasts.

Normandy Chicken with Calvados Cream Sauce

A perfect dish for a special dinner party. The time consuming preparation may be done in advance.

CHICKEN:

½ cup minced onion

4 tablespoons unsalted butter

1 Golden Delicious apple, peeled, cored and chopped

½ teaspoon crumbled sage

½ teaspoon crumbled thyme

Salt and freshly ground black pepper, to taste

2 teaspoons fresh lemon juice

4 whole chicken breasts, split, boned and skinned

All purpose flour for dredging

2 eggs beaten with 2 teaspoons water

½ cup fine dry bread crumbs

½ cup finely chopped almonds

¼ cup vegetable oil

SAUCE:

½ cup minced onion

¼ cup dry white wine

¼ cup apple cider

1 cup chicken stock

1 cup heavy cream

2 tablespoons Calvados

- TO PREPARE THE CHICKEN: Sauté the onion in butter over medium heat, stirring until softened.

- Add the apple, sage, thyme, salt and pepper.

- Cook the mixture for 10 minutes, covered, or until apple is tender.

- Stir in the lemon juice and let the mixture cool.

- Lightly pound the chicken breasts between wax paper until ¼"thick.

- Place 2 tablespoons of filling on each chicken breast and fold to close. If necessary use toothpicks to secure.

- Combine bread crumbs and almonds.

- Dredge the chicken in flour, dip in egg mixture and then in the crumb-almond mixture.

- Chill the chicken for at least one hour or overnight, covered.

- Preheat oven to 350°F.

Continued on next page

- In a heavy skillet, heat oil over moderate heat, brown the breasts, then transfer them to a baking pan and bake for 20 minutes.

- TO PREPARE THE SAUCE: In a medium-size saucepan, combine the onion, wine and cider and boil until almost all the liquid is evaporated.

- Add the stock and boil until reduced by ½.

- Add the cream and Calvados and boil the sauce until it is thickened slightly.

- Pour sauce over chicken. Serve immediately.

4 – 6 SERVINGS

Note: May be prepared in advance up to cooking the chicken.

Chicken Breasts Provencal

Tomatoes with chicken is a classic French recipe. The rich sauce has a savory aroma.

4 chicken breasts, split, boned and skinned

Salt and freshly ground black pepper, to taste

½ cup all purpose flour

4 – 5 tablespoons unsalted butter

1 – 2 tablespoons olive oil

⅓ cup Cognac

1 tablespoon minced scallions

1 garlic clove, minced

6 ripe tomatoes, peeled, seeded, juiced and chopped

1 tablespoon basil, chopped or 1 teaspoon dried

½ cup dry white wine

½ cup chicken stock

½ cup heavy cream

3 tablespoons chopped fresh parsley

- Season chicken with salt and pepper and dredge lightly with flour.

- Melt 2 tablespoons butter and 1 tablespoon oil in large skillet until butter foams and begins to subside, but not browned.

- Sauté breasts one layer at a time until lightly browned on each side.

- Remove breasts as they are done and continue with the rest adding more oil and butter if necessary to keep the pan filmed.

- Return all the chicken to the pan.

- Over high heat pour in Cognac and when bubbling ignite with long-handled match. Remember to avert your face.

- Shake pan for several seconds.

- Remove contents of pan to another dish.

- Add another tablespoon of butter and stir in scallions and garlic and cook for a moment.

- Add tomatoes and basil and cook for 5 minutes or until tomatoes begin to cook.

- Pour in wine, stock and cream and boil for several minutes until sauce thickens.

- Taste and correct seasonings.

- Return chicken to pan and baste.

- Garnish with parsley and serve.

6 – 8 SERVINGS

Country Chicken with Artichokes

2½ pounds chicken parts

2 tablespoons butter or margarine

Salt and freshly ground black pepper, to taste

1 garlic clove, minced

1 bay leaf

¼ teaspoon marjoram

¼ teaspoon thyme

¾ cup chicken broth

¾ cup dry white wine

1 cup fresh or frozen small white onions, defrosted if frozen

1½ cups fresh or frozen baby carrots, defrosted if frozen

9 ounces artichoke hearts, canned or frozen, defrosted, halved

⅓ cup country Dijon mustard

1 tablespoon all purpose flour (optional)

2 tablespoons water (optional)

- In a large skillet, brown chicken in butter in a large skillet. Season with salt and pepper.

- Add garlic, bay leaf, marjoram, thyme, chicken broth and wine.

- Simmer, covered, 35 minutes, stirring occasionally.

- Add the onions, carrots and artichokes. Simmer, covered, until vegetables are tender, about 10 minutes.

- Remove chicken and vegetables to a heated serving platter.

- Add mustard to remaining liquid and bring to a boil.

- If desired, thicken sauce with a mixture of flour and water.

- Spoon sauce over chicken and vegetables.

- Serve immediately.

6 SERVINGS

Note: May be prepared in advance up to thickening sauce. Reheat. Do not freeze. Recipe may be doubled.

A very colorful and hearty meal. Serve with roasted garlic potatoes.

Orange Tarragon Chicken Breasts

The orange juice and tarragon combine to give a sweet and interesting flavor.

This recipe is very quick and easy to prepare.

2 cups freshly squeezed orange juice

1 cup chicken stock or canned chicken broth

2 teaspoons chopped fresh or 1 teaspoon dried tarragon

2 whole chicken breasts, split, skinned, boned and pounded thin

Salt and freshly ground black pepper, to taste

2 tablespoons unsalted butter

GARNISH:

Orange sections

- In a large skillet bring orange juice, chicken broth and tarragon to a boil.
- Season chicken breasts with salt and pepper and add to skillet.
- Cook chicken for 2 minutes per side over medium-high heat.
- Remove chicken from pan and set aside.
- Reduce orange juice and chicken broth mixture to approximately 4 tablespoons of liquid, about 5 – 10 minutes.
- Remove pan from heat and stir in butter until melted.
- Return chicken to the pan and heat 1 minute on each side.
- Remove chicken from pan with slotted spoon and arrange on a heated serving platter.
- Spoon sauce over chicken and serve immediately.
- Garnish with small orange sections.

4 SERVINGS

Note: Recipe may be doubled and frozen.

Old South Meeting House

Old State House

Old State House

Located at the intersection of State and Washington Streets in the heart of Boston is the Old State House, standing proudly among towering modern-day office buildings. Long ago, this was the site of a public market, a center buzzing with life and commerce. The two main roads at that time were known as King Street and the Road to the Neck. In the surrounding area were the homes of famous Bostonians including Governor John Winthrop and Captain Robert Keayne. It was Captain Keayne who bequeathed the funds to build the first building upon this site in 1657. It was known as the Town House. Unfortunately, it burned down in the Great Fire of 1711.

In 1713, the two-story structure with cupola was built as the seat of the King's Colonial Government. At the eastern end of the Old State House were the golden lion and unicorn, symbols of the King of England. The Royal Government conducted its business here until hastily leaving in 1764.

In front of the Old State House, the first American lives were given in the cause of the revolution in 1770 in the Boston Massacre.

The Old State House became the seat of government for the fledgling Commonwealth of Massachusetts in 1776. A large American eagle was placed at the western end of the building. During the same year, from the Old State House balcony, John Hancock read the Declaration of Independence to the large crowd assembled below. The lion and unicorn were torn down at this time to symbolize the end of tyranny. Today these statues have been replicated and remounted atop the building.

The Old State House is now a museum of Boston history maintained by the Bostonian Society.

Orange Glazed Pork Medallions

Thin orange slices can be used to garnish this tasty dish. Serve with fried rice for an oriental touch.

5 tablespoons frozen concentrated orange juice, defrosted

3 tablespoons Dijon mustard

2 garlic cloves, chopped

¼ teaspoon ground ginger

¼ teaspoon white pepper

6½ tablespoons olive oil, divided

6 boneless pork chops

1 cup sliced almonds

2 cups chicken broth

1 teaspoon cornstarch in 1 tablespoon water

2 tablespoons orange marmalade

2 tablespoons butter, cut into pieces

2 tablespoons chopped fresh parsley

¼ teaspoon red pepper flakes

- Beat orange juice concentrate, mustard, garlic, ginger and pepper in 5 tablespoons olive oil.

- Marinate pork in the mixture for 1 hour at room temperature.

- Sauté almonds in ½ tablespoon oil. Remove and set aside.

- Drain pork, reserving marinade.

- In large skillet, cook pork over high heat in 1 tablespoon oil for 6 – 10 minutes. Remove pork from pan.

- Strain marinade into pan. Add chicken broth and cornstarch mixture.

- Cook over high heat, stirring occasionally, until sauce reduces by slightly more than half, about 5 minutes.

- Add marmalade and stir over medium heat to melt.

- Over high heat, stir in butter, parsley and red pepper.

- Add pork and heat through.

- Add almonds and stir.

6 SERVINGS

Barbecued Butterfly Lamb

MARINADE:

1 cup red wine

½ cup vegetable oil

2 tablespoons chopped fresh parsley

2 tablespoons chives

½ teaspoon Worcestershire sauce

¼ teaspoon freshly ground black pepper

⅛ teaspoon marjoram

⅛ teaspoon rosemary

⅛ teaspoon thyme

2 garlic cloves, minced

1 teaspoon salt

1 leg of lamb, boned and flattened

- TO PREPARE THE MARINADE: Combine wine, oil, parsley, chives, Worcestershire sauce, pepper, marjoram, rosemary, thyme, garlic and salt.

- Pour marinade over lamb in non-metalic dish and cover well. Marinate lamb overnight in refrigerator, turning periodically.

- Preheat grill. Barbecue for 15 minutes or until done, basting with marinade.

6 – 8 SERVINGS

The seasoning is authoritative and fragrant. Serve with a simple green salad and garlic roasted sweet potatoes.

Steak with Mustard Sauce

2 boneless strip steaks

3 tablespoons butter, divided

2 shallots, finely chopped

1 tablespoon Dijon mustard

½ cup dry white wine

2 teaspoons finely chopped fresh parsley

- Remove all fat from steaks. Pound until they are ¼″ – ½″ thick.

- In hot skillet, sear steaks approximately 2 – 3 minutes on each side.

- Remove steaks to warmed platter and pour off excess fat leaving a thin film only.

- Add 1 tablespoon butter and sauté shallots over moderate heat until soft but not colored.

- Stir mustard into wine, deglaze the pan with this mixture and reduce until the sauce is thickened.

- Add parsley and whisk in remaining butter. Serve immediately.

2 SERVINGS

Very quick and simple.

The sauce is rich and indulgent.

The Dijon mustard lends piquancy to an otherwise basic steak.

Pasta Mushroom Italian

A very hearty and spicy vegetarian pasta. Serve with a green salad and crusty Italian bread.

2 pounds fresh plum tomatoes

¼ cup olive oil

1 12-ounce package fresh mushrooms, coarsely sliced

1 teaspoon salt

1 tablespoon savory

2 teaspoons thyme

1 teaspoon marjoram

1 teaspoon freshly ground black pepper

¼ cup tomato paste

10 – 15 ounces fresh pasta – hot red pepper fettucini or linguine is perfect

⅓ cup freshly grated Romano cheese

1 pound pasta

- Bring a large pot of salted water to a full boil.
- Drop tomatoes, one layer at a time, into water.
- Scald until skin begins to split. With slotted spoon, transfer to a bowl and slip off skin.
- Repeat with remaining tomatoes.
- Core tomatoes and coarsely chop.
- Heat oil in heavy saucepan over medium-high heat.
- Add mushrooms; sauté uncovered for 10 minutes until softened, not limp.
- Add salt, savory, thyme, marjoram and pepper.
- Add tomatoes and tomato paste, and stir well.
- Cook over low heat, stirring constantly for 15 minutes, to reduce liquid slightly. Do not burn bottom. Do not cover.
- Correct seasonings in sauce.
- Prepare pasta per directions on package.
- To serve, spoon sauce over pasta and sprinkle with Romano cheese.

2 – 3 SERVINGS

Marinated Pork Tenderloin Grill

MARINADE:

3 garlic cloves, crushed

1 cup chopped onions (add ½ cup for stronger onion flavor)

½ cup fresh lemon juice

½ cup soy sauce

½ cup vegetable oil

⅛ cup granulated sugar

3 tablespoons chopped cilantro (Chinese parsley)

Splash of hot red pepper sauce

4 – 6 pork tenderloins, approximately 3 pounds (A butcher will prepare this cut of pork)

- TO MAKE THE MARINADE: In a large non-metallic dish, mix well the garlic, onions, lemon juice, soy sauce, oil, sugar, cilantro and hot pepper sauce. Make sure the tenderloins fit in one layer.

- Place tenderloins in marinade for 8 – 12 hours, turning periodically.

- Preheat grill.

- When grill is hot, cook tenderloins, basting with marinade.

- Grill 10 – 12 minutes per side until done.

- Slice and serve immediately.

6 – 8 SERVINGS

Note: It is important to marinate the pork for 8 – 12 hours for tenderness. When cooked make sure pork turns whitish and is completely done.

This is a great party dish. The marinating is done in advance, leaving the hosts to their guests. The marinade is simple but delicious. Chicken or shrimp may be substituted for pork.

Veal Roast with Pistachio Pesto Stuffing On Toasted Couscous

Couscous plays the same role in a menu as rice. It is made from durum wheat semolina. The neutral flavor makes it a good partner for many foods.

STUFFING:

½ cup shelled pistachio nuts

1 medium size bunch watercress (reserve a few sprigs for garnish)

½ cup freshly grated Parmesan cheese

3 tablespoons olive oil

¾ teaspoon salt

One 3½ pound rolled boneless veal leg sirloin roast with fat covering

TOASTED COUSCOUS:

1 package (14 ounces) couscous (precooked semolina)

3 cups boiling water

½ teaspoon salt

6 tablespoons butter

1 medium onion, chopped

GRAVY:

1½ cups water

2 tablespoons flour

- Preheat oven to 325°F.

- TO PREPARE THE STUFFING: Coarsely chop enough nuts to measure 1 tablespoon. Reserve for garnish.

- In food processor using knife blade, blend remaining nuts, watercress, cheese, oil and salt until consistency of a paste. Stop occasionally to scrape down sides.

- TO STUFF THE ROAST: Untie veal and place fat side on work surface. Using a sharp knife, slice the roast horizontally, keeping the knife parallel to the cutting surface. Start at the long side and cut almost but not all the way through. Spread open the roast, making a rectangle about 14″ × 8″. Pound veal with mallet to make it about 1″ thick throughout.

- Spread the stuffing evenly over the roast. Starting at the narrow end, carefully roll the veal, jellyroll fashion. Fasten with skewers and re-tie about every 2″.

- Place roast, fat side up, on roasting rack in pan. Insert meat thermometer. Roast until thermometer reads 170°F., about 2 hours. Remove from oven.

Continued on next page

- TO PREPARE THE COUSCOUS: About 30 minutes before veal will be ready, stir couscous, water and salt together. Let stand for 5 minutes.

- Spread mixture on large plate to cool for 15 minutes.

- In medium size skillet, melt butter and add onion.

- Cook until onion is lightly browned over medium-high heat.

- Add the couscous and cook over high heat for about 10 minutes until lightly browned and toasted, stirring often. Keep warm.

- TO PREPARE THE GRAVY: Remove roast from pan and skim off all fat from pan.

- In small bowl, mix water and flour. Stir into pan drippings and cook over medium heat, stirring until gravy boils and thickens. Pour into gravy bowl.

- Remove strings and skewers. Slice roast into thin slices.

- Arrange slices of veal on top of couscous on platter. Serve gravy on the side. Garnish with watercress and reserved chopped nuts.

12 SERVINGS

Veal with Water Chestnuts and Mushrooms

A very sophisticated veal dish. An unusual combination of flavors and textures.

1 stick butter

2 pounds of boneless veal, cubed

1 clove garlic

1 medium onion, grated

1 teaspoon salt

¼ teaspoon freshly ground pepper

Dash cayenne

1 pound fresh mushrooms, quartered

1 cup light beef bouillon

⅛ teaspoon nutmeg

1 bay leaf

1 can sliced water chestnuts

¼ cup cognac

1 cup heavy cream

1 tablespoon chopped parsley

- Preheat oven to 350°F.

- Melt 4 tablespoons of butter in a heavy skillet.

- Brown veal on all sides. Add garlic and onion toward the end to brown along with the meat.

- When meat is brown, season with salt, pepper and cayenne and place in a covered heat-proof dish.

- In skillet, melt the remaining 4 tablespoons of butter. Sauté the quartered mushrooms quickly, stirring to cook evenly. Add to the meat.

- Deglaze the skillet with a little of the beef bouillon. Add to the meat and mushrooms along with the remaining beef bouillon.

- Add nutmeg, bay leaf and water chestnuts. Stir, cover and place in oven. Cook until meat is tender, about 1 hour.

- Add cream. Stir and cook uncovered 15 minutes.

- Add cognac; reheat. Sprinkle with parsley and serve.

6 SERVINGS

Note: May be prepared in advance up to the point of adding the cream.

Winter Barbecued Spareribs

3 pounds spareribs or 2 pounds boneless country ribs,
   separated

¾ cup ketchup

¼ cup brown sugar

1 tablespoon Worcestershire sauce

2 teaspoons dry mustard

¼ cup cider or red wine vinegar

¼ cup maple syrup

¼ cup minced fresh or 2 tablespoons dried onion

Salt and freshly ground black pepper, to taste

3 cups prepared white rice

- Sear ribs in a dutch oven without oil over medium-high heat on top of stove.

- Reduce heat to medium-low.

- In a medium bowl, mix ketchup, brown sugar, Worcestershire sauce, mustard, vinegar, maple syrup and onion.

- Pour mixture over ribs and simmer over low heat for 2½ – 3 hours, stirring occasionally.

- Season with salt and pepper.

- Serve over white rice.

4 SERVINGS

A very simple barbecue recipe that can be made year round on top of the stove.

Sticky and sweet, the meat melts off the rib bones.

French Country Pork Chops

This is a meal in itself. Meat and potatoes combined.

POTATOES:

8 – 10 small new potatoes

4 tablespoons unsalted butter

Salt and freshly ground black pepper, to taste

CHOPS:

6 pork chops

Salt and freshly ground black pepper, to taste

Flour for dredging

Unsalted butter for dredging

2 strips bacon

3 medium onions, peeled and diced

1 cup beef bouillon

¼ cup dry white wine

2 tablespoons tomato paste

GARNISH:

Minced fresh parsley

- TO PREPARE THE POTATOES: Wash and drop in boiling water to cover.

- Cook approximately 20 minutes after water returns to boil.

- Drain potatoes and cool.

- Cut potatoes into wedges and sauté in butter until browned.

- Sprinkle with salt and pepper. Set aside.

- Preheat oven to 350°F.

- TO PREPARE THE CHOPS: Sprinkle with salt and pepper and dust with flour.

- Cook bacon until it starts to render fat. Add the onion and chops and enough butter to cook onions and brown chops well on both sides.

- Add bouillon, wine and paste.

- Bake at 350°F. uncovered.

- When ready to serve, add the potatoes and spoon the sauce over the meat.

- Sprinkle with parsley and serve hot.

6 SERVINGS

Note: As an alternative to baking, recipe can be cooked on stove top until chops are tender, about 30 minutes.

Aromatic Orange Pork Ka-bobs

MARINADE:

½ teaspoon whole black peppercorns, crushed

2 tablespoons grated fresh orange rind

½ cup orange juice concentrate, defrosted

1 tablespoon Honeycup mustard

¼ cup red wine vinegar

1 tablespoon honey

¼ teaspoon thyme

One 2″ piece cinnamon stick

1½ – 2 pounds pork loin, cubed

- TO PREPARE THE MARINADE: In medium saucepan, combine pepper, orange rind, orange juice, mustard, vinegar, honey and thyme. Bring to a boil, stirring constantly.

- Remove from heat and add cinnamon stick. Cool.

- Pour over pork in shallow non-metallic dish. Cover and marinate 8 – 12 hours.

- Preheat grill or broiler. Cook, basting with marinade, until done.

4 SERVINGS

The scent of orange cinnamon fills the air while grilling these tasty ka-bobs.

Serve on a bed of ORANGE RICE.

Teriyaki Steak

¼ cup soy sauce

3 tablespoons honey

2 tablespoons red wine vinegar

1 teaspoon garlic powder

1½ teaspoons ground ginger

¾ cup vegetable oil

1 finely chopped green onion, white and green parts

1 flank or top round steak to serve 4

- TO PREPARE THE MARINADE: Mix soy sauce, honey, vinegar, garlic powder, ginger, oil and green onion together.

- Pour marinade over steak in non-metallic dish and cover well. Refrigerate 8 – 12 hours, turning periodically.

- Preheat broiler or grill. Cook 5 minutes on each side, or until done.

4 SERVINGS

A flavorful all purpose teriyaki marinade. Versatile enough for shrimp or ribs.

Cognac Glazed Lamb Chops

A flavorful sauce that gives the chops a shiny glaze. Perfect for an elegant dinner party.

Bourbon can be substituted for cognac for a stronger flavor.

Serve with DUCHESS SWEET POTATO and SUMMER SQUASH CUPS WITH PEAS.

½ cup dry red wine

½ cup unsalted beef broth

2 tablespoons vegetable oil

8 1" thick loin lamb chops

Salt and freshly ground black pepper, to taste

2 tablespoons minced shallots

2 garlic cloves, minced

¼ cup cognac

1 teaspoon Worcestershire sauce

1½ sticks unsalted butter, chilled and cut into tablespoon size pieces

GARNISH:

Minced fresh parsley or watercress leaves

- In a small saucepan, simmer wine and broth until reduced to ½ cup.

- Heat oil in large heavy skillet over high heat.

- Add lamb to skillet and cook approximately 4 minutes on each side until medium-rare.

- Season to taste with salt and pepper. Transfer chops to warm platter.

- Pour off all but 1 tablespoon of fat in skillet.

- Add shallots and garlic and cook until translucent over medium heat.

- Add cognac and Worcestershire sauce. Bring to boil over high heat, scraping up all browned bits in skillet.

- Add wine mixture to skillet and boil until reduced to ¼ cup liquid.

- Remove pan from heat and whisk in 2 tablespoons butter at a time until all butter is incorporated. (Return pan to medium heat if sauce breaks down.)

- Whisk any liquid on lamb platter into sauce.

- Spoon sauce over lamb chops. Serve immediately.

- Garnish with parsley or watercress.

4 – 6 SERVINGS

Pork with Spiced Peaches

8 thin boneless pork chops

1 teaspoon salt

1 teaspoon freshly ground black pepper

2 tablespoons butter

1 can (29 ounces) sliced Cling peaches with syrup

1 cup brown sugar

¾ cup apple cider vinegar

⅛ teaspoon freshly grated nutmeg

1 teaspoon thyme

- Preheat broiler.
- Season pork chops with salt and pepper.
- In a heavy large skillet, heat butter. Add pork and sauté over medium heat until golden brown, about 3 minutes on each side.
- Transfer pork to warmed, heat-proof platter.
- Drain peaches, reserving syrup.
- In saucepan, mix syrup, brown sugar, vinegar, nutmeg and thyme.
- Heat to boiling. Reduce heat and simmer until slightly thickened.
- Stir in sliced peaches and cook 5 minutes longer.
- Pour sauce over pork chops.
- Place platter under broiler until lightly browned and bubbly.

4 – 6 SERVINGS

Sweet and peachy.

Serve with wild rice for nutty contrast.

Tenderloin of Beef

A beef tenderloin is also called the "filet." It can be cooked whole or cut into small steaks (filets mignons).

Ask the butcher to remove the ends so that the tenderloin will be an even thickness.

5 – 6 pound tenderloin of beef, trimmed, peeled and tied

1½ tablespoons Kosher salt

1 tablespoon freshly ground black pepper

2 tablespoons olive oil

- Preheat oven to 450°F.

- Sprinkle tenderloin with salt and pepper.

- Place a large skillet over high heat and add the oil. When very hot, sear the meat on all sides, turning often.

- Set a rack inside a roasting pan and place beef on the rack. Insert a meat thermometer into the beef.

- Roast in the oven for 15 – 20 minutes or until 110°F. on the meat thermometer, indicating rare beef. (120°F. for medium rare beef.).

- Allow tenderloin to rest for 10 minutes before slicing.

- Serve with Horseradish Sauce.

Horseradish Sauce

1 cup whipped cream

3 tablespoons prepared white horseradish, squeezed dry

1 teaspoon Dijon mustard

- Fold horseradish into whipped cream.
- Add mustard and serve.

Boston Massacre Site

Along-side the Old State House on Washington Street is a ring of cobblestones. These mark the site of the Boston Massacre, that fateful skirmish which claimed the first lives of the Revolution.

On a snowy March 5, 1770, a group of colonists provoked a fight with a detachment of nine British troops. It began when a colonist pelted one British soldier with snowballs, sticks and ice. Soon the area was crowded with British troops and colonial townsmen. The harassment continued until one British soldier broke down and fired into the crowd. Five colonists were killed including Crispus Attucks, an early black patriot to die for the cause of independence. Blood had been shed and the colonists were incensed.

In the weeks and months to come the "massacre" became a rallying point for the colonists. Each year this event was commemorated as the night "our streets were stained with the Blood of our Brethren, our ears were wounded by the groans of the dying, and our eyes were tormented with the sight of the mangled bodies of the Dead."

Linguine with Lobster and Tomato Sauce

An elegant and delicious way to serve lobster. The spicy tomato and brandy sauce is a perfect compliment.

Lobsters have not always been the luxury they are today. In Colonial times they were used as fertilizer.

¼ cup olive oil

½ tablespoon minced garlic

½ cup chopped sweet red peppers

3½ – 4 cups crushed canned plum tomatoes, undrained (32 ounces)

1 tablespoon chopped fresh parsley

½ teaspoon hot red pepper flakes

¼ teaspoon freshly ground black pepper

2 teaspoons oregano

2 tablespoons fresh or 2 teaspoons dried basil

¼ cup brandy

2 cans (11.3 ounces each) frozen lobster meat, thawed and drained*

1½ pounds linguine

- Heat oil in heavy skillet, add garlic and peppers and cook over medium heat until peppers soften.

- Add tomatoes, parsley, hot pepper flakes, pepper, oregano and basil. Bring to a boil, reduce heat and simmer uncovered for 30 minutes.

- Add brandy and return to a boil.

- Add lobster meat, reduce heat to low and cook gently until lobster is cooked through, about 5 minutes.

- Cook linguine al dente, drain and serve with lobster and tomato sauce.

4 – 6 SERVINGS

* Can use fresh lobster meat from 3 live 2-pound lobsters, cooked in 1″ salted boiling water for 20 minutes, cooled and shelled.

Orangy Snapper

6 (4 ounce) red snapper or other fish fillets

3 tablespoons water

2 tablespoons frozen orange juice concentrate, thawed and undiluted

2 teaspoons olive oil

½ teaspoon freshly grated orange rind

Dash of freshly ground black pepper

Dash of freshly grated nutmeg

GARNISH:

Orange wedges

Parsley sprigs

- Preheat oven to 350°F.

- Place fillets in a 12″ × 8″ × 2″ heat-proof baking dish coated with cooking spray.

- Combine water, juice concentrate, oil and grated orange rind in a small bowl, stirring well.

- Pour over fillets, then sprinkle with pepper and nutmeg.

- Bake uncovered for 20 – 25 minutes or until fish flakes easily when tested with a fork.

- Garnish with orange wedges and parsley.

6 SERVINGS

Note: Scrod, haddock or flounder can be substituted for the snapper.

Add 1 teaspoon freshly grated gingerroot to the sauce for an oriental zip.

Do not include any of the white pith when grating the orange rind; it will be bitter.

Spicy Blackened Swordfish

A hot and sassy fish dish from the Big Easy.

2 tablespoons chopped garlic

2 tablespoons chopped onion

1 teaspoon white pepper

1 teaspoon thyme

1 teaspoon basil

1 teaspoon oregano

4 teaspoons paprika

1½ teaspoons cayenne pepper

1 teaspoon ground cumin

¼ teaspoon ground ginger

½ teaspoon salt

2 tablespoons chicken base granules (chicken broth in powdered form)

1 stick butter, melted

4 swordfish steaks, 6 – 7 ounces each

- Preheat oven to 350°F.

- Mix together garlic, onion, pepper, thyme, basil, oregano, paprika, cayenne, cumin, ginger, salt and chicken base granules.

- Coat fish with seasoning, then coat in butter.

- Place in a smoking hot iron skillet for approximately 1 minute on each side.

- Bake in hot iron skillet in the oven until flaky.

4 SERVINGS

Seafood Au Gratin

1 large bay leaf

2 stalks celery, halved

3 – 4 crushed black peppercorns

1 pound medium shrimp

1 pound bay scallops

5 tablespoons butter

1 garlic clove, minced

3 large shallots, minced

½ pound mushrooms, sliced

¼ cup all purpose flour

1 tablespoon minced fresh or 1 teaspoon dried dill

¾ cup light cream

¾ cup dry white wine

2 cups grated Monterey Jack cheese

Salt and freshly ground black pepper, to taste

1 package (9 ounces) frozen artichoke hearts, cooked and drained

¼ cup soft fresh bread crumbs

A sensational entrée. Rich and satisfying.

- Preheat oven to 375°F.

- In a large saucepan, bring 2 quarts of water, the bay leaf, celery and peppercorns to a boil. Add the shrimp and cook for 3 minutes, or until the shrimp shells are pink.

- Remove the shrimp with a slotted spoon, peel, devein and set aside.

- Add the scallops to the cooking water and bring to a boil. Immediately reduce the heat. Poach the scallops until just opaque, about 1 minute. Remove and set aside.

- In a large skillet, melt the butter and sauté the garlic and shallots for 2 – 3 minutes over medium heat. Add the mushrooms and sauté until lightly browned, about 5 minutes.

- Add the flour and dill and cook until well blended. Add the cream and wine and cook, stirring until thick.

- Add half the cheese and season to taste with salt and pepper. Stir until smooth.

- Add the shrimp, scallops and artichokes to the sauce and mix.

- Pour the gratin mixture into a buttered, shallow heat-proof dish. Top with bread crumbs and remaining cheese.

- Bake 25 – 30 minutes or until bubbly and light brown.

6 – 8 SERVINGS

Seafood Pasta Salad

This satisfying salad is bright and crunchy with surprises. Very portable.

SALAD:

1 pound pasta in a variety of shapes: shells, twists or corkscrews, cooked al dente and drained

3 cups seafood: a combination of white fish, shrimp, mussels, sea scallops, lobster, crab, cooked until tender, chopped and drained

¾ cup ripe plum tomatoes, halved and seeded

¼ cup chopped fresh parsley

3 tablespoons coarsely chopped fresh basil leaves

¼ cup chopped pimientos

1 cup chopped fresh dill

½ cup chopped shallots

3 tablespoons capers, drained

¼ cup black olives, pitted and chopped

¼ cup grated fresh zucchini, drained

VINAIGRETTE:

½ cup fresh lemon juice

1 tablespoon red wine vinegar

½ cup olive oil

¼ cup Dijon mustard

- In a large bowl, toss pasta, seafood, tomatoes, parsley, basil, pimientos, dill, shallots, capers, olives and zucchini.

- TO PREPARE THE VINAIGRETTE: In a small bowl, whisk together the lemon juice, vinegar, olive oil and mustard.

- Toss the vinaigrette with the salad to taste, to coat lightly.

- Taste and correct seasoning if necessary.

- Refrigerate several hours to allow flavors to blend.

- Serve well chilled.

6 – 8 SERVINGS

Note: If salad is refrigerated overnight, it may be moistened with remaining viniagrette.

Salmon Steaks with Broccoli Mousse and Hollandaise Sauce

6 small salmon steaks, ½"
thick

1 package (10 ounces) frozen
chopped broccoli

6 egg whites

1½ teaspoons minced fresh
or ½ teaspoon dried
tarragon

¼ teaspoon salt

SAUCE:

6 egg yolks

¼ cup fresh lemon juice

½ teaspoon salt

2 sticks butter, melted

GARNISH:

Lemon slices

- Preheat oven to 375°F. Grease a jelly roll pan.

- Cut each steak along center bone into 2 pieces, discard bones. On jelly roll pan, reassemble fish pieces into original shape, wrapping ends slightly around each other to leave a small opening.

- Prepare broccoli as directed on package, drain and cool.

- TO PREPARE THE MOUSSE: In food processor using knife blade or blender at low speed, blend broccoli, egg whites, tarragon and salt until mixture is smooth.

- Mound mousse in opening of each steak.

- Bake 15 minutes or until fish flakes easily when tested with a fork. Remove from oven and keep warm.

- TO PREPARE THE SAUCE: In food processor using a knife blade, or blender at low speed, blend egg yolks, lemon juice and salt until smooth and thick.

- Remove center of cover and, at high speed, pour hot butter very slowly in a steady stream into egg mixture. Continue until well mixed.

- To serve, pour hollandaise sauce onto platter or individual plate. With slotted spatula remove each steak from pan, drain over paper towels and arrange on top of the sauce. Garnish with lemon slices.

6 SERVINGS

An impressive and delicious way to serve salmon. Well worth the effort.

Mussels Provencale

The lowly mussel has risen to great heights in this classic French dish.

Did you know that the Neptune Shell has been officially proclaimed the shell of Massachusetts?

¼ cup chopped onion

¼ cup chopped celery

3 garlic cloves, crushed

½ cup olive oil

½ cup dry white wine or French vermouth

1 tablespoon fresh lemon juice

1 28-ounce can crushed Italian tomatoes

¼ cup chopped parsley

1 teaspoon basil

⅛ teaspoon freshly ground black pepper

1 teaspoon salt

3 dozen or approximately 3 pounds of medium size mussels which have been cleaned and soaked in cold water with a handful of cornmeal for 1 hour

1 pound pasta

GARNISH:

¼ cup chopped parsley

- In a heavy saucepan with a lid to fit, sauté onion, celery and garlic in olive oil for 10 minutes uncovered, until transparent.

- Add wine, lemon juice, tomatoes, parsley, basil and salt and pepper to taste.

- Bring to a boil, reduce heat and simmer for 1 minute.

- Add the prepared mussels, cover pan and cook over high heat 5 – 8 minutes, shaking pan frequently. Do not serve any mussels that have not opened.

- Cook pasta in boiling water, al dente.

- Spoon mussels and sauce over pasta. Sprinkle with reserved parsley. Serve immediately.

4 SERVINGS

Grilled Salmon Steaks with Tarragon Butter

4 tablespoons butter or margarine, softened

1 shallot, minced

1 tablespoon chopped fresh or 1 teaspoon dried tarragon

1 tablespoon chopped fresh or 1 teaspoon dried chives

1½ teaspoons chopped fresh or ½ teaspoon dried parsley

⅛ teaspoon freshly ground black pepper

1 tablespoon Dijon mustard

4 salmon steaks, 1½" thick

- Preheat grill.
- Combine butter, shallot, tarragon, chives, parsley, pepper and mustard mixing well. Brush salmon steaks with butter mixture.
- Cook over hot grill, brushing frequently with remaining butter mixture, 8 minutes on each side or until fish flakes easily when tested with fork.

4 SERVINGS

Note: Tarragon butter can be prepared in advance.

The tarragon butter gives these rich steaks a subtle flavor. Very simple and flavorful.

Grilled Marinated Swordfish

3 pounds swordfish steaks

⅓ cup soy sauce

¼ cup fresh lemon juice

½ cup vegetable oil

1 large garlic clove, crushed

1 teaspoon grated lemon rind

2 teaspoons Dijon mustard

½ cup chopped fresh parsley

- Pierce swordfish steaks on each side with a fork. Place in a shallow non-metallic dish.
- In a medium bowl, combine soy sauce, lemon juice, oil, garlic, lemon rind, mustard and parsley. Pour over fish. Marinate covered in the refrigerator for 3 – 24 hours, turning the fish occasionally.
- Preheat grill.
- Remove the fish from the marinade. Reserve the marinade.
- Grill or broil the fish approximately 6 – 8 minutes per side, basting with the reserved marinade, just until fish flakes easily when tested with a fork. Serve immediately.

6 SERVINGS

This fresh grilled swordfish needs little adornment other than a refreshing fruit salad with tangy dressing.

The fish will be tender, moist and smoky-sweet.

Scallops Nantucket

This rich and tasty dish is fantastic for either an appetizer or main entrée.

Nantucket Bay Scallops are the ultimate in scallops.

2 pounds bay scallops

2 cups dry white wine

6 shallots, minced

Juice of 1 lemon

1 bay leaf

½ teaspoon thyme

Salt and freshly ground black pepper, to taste

2 tablespoons butter

2 tablespoons flour

2 cups heavy cream

1 pound mushrooms, sliced thin

6 puffed pastry shells

- Poach scallops in wine until translucent and slightly undercooked.

- Refrigerate scallops, reserving poaching liquid for sauce.

- In a medium saucepan, add shallots, lemon juice, bay leaf, thyme, salt and pepper to poaching liquid.

- Simmer for 30 minutes.

- In a small skillet, melt butter. Stir in flour to form a roux, gently cooking until golden.

- Whisk roux into liquid poaching mixture gradually until it thickens, cooking and stirring.

- Add heavy cream.

- In a large skillet, strain sauce over scallops and uncooked mushrooms.

- Simmer 5 minutes.

- Serve over pastry shells.

6 SERVINGS

Grilled Bluefish with Anchovy Mustard Sauce

4 bluefish steaks, about ½ pound each

1½ teaspoons fresh lemon juice

1 teaspoon caper juice

3 tablespoons olive oil

2 tablespoons chopped fresh or 2 teaspoons dried dill

2 tablespoons butter

2 tablespoons all purpose flour

½ cup water

¼ cup white wine

1 teaspoon anchovy paste

1 tablespoon Dijon mustard

2 tablespoons crushed capers

Salt and freshly ground black pepper, to taste

1 cup sour cream

- Arrange bluefish in a shallow, non-metalic dish.
- Mix lemon juice, caper juice, olive oil and dill and pour over fish.
- Marinate fish covered in the refrigerator for 2 hours.
- Preheat grill.
- TO PREPARE THE SAUCE: In small saucepan, melt butter, add flour and cook gently. Remove from heat.
- Stir water and wine into butter mixture. Return to low heat and cook until mixture thickens.
- Stir anchovy paste, mustard and capers into butter mixture and continue to cook.
- Add salt and pepper.
- Grill fish over coals slowly until fork can be inserted easily, about 15 minutes.
- Serve with sauce and a dollop of sour cream.

4 SERVINGS

Bluefish abound along the Massachusetts shore each summer.

The marinating removes any oily flavors and gives a distinct tangy zest to the fish.

Shrimp Scampi

36 large fresh shrimp in shells*

¾ cup clarified butter

¼ cup virgin olive oil

2 tablespoons minced garlic

2 tablespoons fresh lemon juice

½ teaspoon dry mustard

1 teaspoon Worcestershire sauce

¼ teaspoon crushed red pepper flakes

1½ teaspoons Italian seasoning

¼ teaspoon salt

2 tablespoons minced fresh Italian parsley

½ cup Chablis or other dry white wine

1 pound linguine verde

GARNISH:

Freshly grated Parmesan cheese

Chopped fresh Italian parsley

- Cut each shrimp ventrally with a sharp, pointed knife, slicing the shrimp from end to end on the underside without cutting through the shell.

- With the pressure of both thumbs on the back side, pop the meat up so it sits on the shell, which is now bent slightly upward in the middle. Set aside.

- In a small saucepan, melt the butter.

- Add oil, garlic, lemon juice, mustard, Worcestershire, red pepper, Italian seasoning, salt and parsley.

- Mix well and simmer over low heat until garlic is blond. Remove from heat.

- Dredge each shrimp in the butter mixture so that it is well coated. Do not discard any sauce that is remaining.

- In a foil-lined shallow pan, arrange the shrimp side by side, flesh side up.

Continued on next page

- Add the Chablis to the butter mixture in saucepan, bring to a boil and simmer for 10 minutes.

- Spoon all the sauce over the shrimp, making certain that garlic bits and herbs cling to the shrimp.

- Preheat the oven to 400°F. and simultaneously bring a pot of salted water to a boil.

- Cook the linguine until it is al dente; drain.

- Bake the shrimp exactly 7 minutes.

- Fork a small mound of pasta in the center of each plate, leaving a small margin around the edge for the shrimp.

- Arrange shrimp with tails pointing outwards at equal intervals around the pasta.

- Spoon the remaining sauce over the pasta and sprinkle with Parmesan and chopped parsley.

6 SERVINGS

* About 25 shrimp to the pound.

Note: *Scampi may be prepared up to baking, then set aside for 1 – 2 hours before finishing.*

Elegant Boston Fish Stew

The ultimate combination of native seafood and shellfish. Serve with crusty bread and a green salad with a tangy vinaigrette.

4 garlic cloves, crushed

1 cup chopped celery

1 cup chopped onion

1 cup chopped green pepper

½ cup olive oil

48 ounces canned tomatoes, chopped, undrained

3 bay leaves

1 tablespoon oregano

½ cup chopped fresh parsley

1 teaspoon red pepper flakes

2 teaspoons salt

1 cup water

3 bottles (8 ounces each) clam juice

1 cup sherry

1 pint oysters, shucked, undrained

1 pound large raw shrimp, shelled and deveined

1 pound fresh, flaked crabmeat

1 pound scrod or any whitefish, chunked

18 littleneck clams, scrubbed

24 mussels, scrubbed

- In 8-quart Dutch oven, sauté garlic, celery, onion and green pepper in oil until limp.

- Add tomatoes, bay leaves, oregano, parsley, red pepper flakes, salt and water. Simmer uncovered 1 hour.

- Add clam juice and sherry. Simmer 10 minutes.

- Add oysters, shrimp, crabmeat and scrod. Simmer 5 minutes.

- Add littlenecks and mussels. Simmer until just open, approximately 5 minutes.

- Serve immediately.

8 SERVINGS

Note: This recipe cannot be microwaved or frozen. May be prepared in advance up to adding seafood.

Faneuil Hall

Located in the old Town Dock area of Boston on State Street, just down the road from the Old State House, is Faneuil Hall, probably Boston's best-known building. At the entrance stands a statue of the famous patriot Samuel Adams. Faneuil Hall was given to the city of Boston in 1742 by the wealthy merchant Peter Faneuil. The two-story structure with the grasshopper weathervane atop the cupola was once the predominant building on Boston's waterfront. The first floor was used as a marketplace, the second for public meetings.

Faneuil Hall was destroyed by fire in 1761 and had to be rebuilt. From that time forth it became the meeting and rallying place for patriots to speak out against the multitude of royal acts that limited their rights and freedoms. Called the Cradle of Liberty, Faneuil Hall was and has always been known for the lively debates and new ideas that emanated from its second-floor meeting room.

In 1805, the Hall was expanded by the addition of a third story designed by Charles Bulfinch. Today the third story hall houses the Ancient and Honorable Artillery Company.

In 1825, landfill began in this area and it soon became desirable commercial real estate. Today, Faneuil Hall, surrounded by Quincy Market shops, restaurants and office buildings, continues to be a vital center visited by thousands of tourists and residents alike.

Summer Squash Cups with Peas

A pretty presentation for a buffet dinner. The contrast of the green peas and the yellow summer squash is dramatic.

5 pounds summer squash, (2½" in diameter) washed and ends trimmed

6 tablespoons butter or margarine, melted, divided

½ cup green onions, minced

2½ cups tiny peas (defrosted if frozen; rinsed and patted dry if fresh)

Salt and freshly ground black pepper, to taste

1 teaspoon fresh lemon juice

1 teaspoon thyme

- Preheat oven to 400°F.

- Peel strips lengthwise from squash to create a striped effect and cut into 2" lengths.

- Hollow out squash lengths from one end with a melon-ball scoop, leaving ¼" sides and ½" bottom.

- Blanch squash in boiling salted water until tender, but firm enough to hold shape, approximately 3 minutes.

- Rinse with cold water and drain.

- Brush squash with 2 tablespoons melted butter and place in a large heat-proof dish.

- Melt remaining 4 tablespoons butter in a large skillet and sauté green onions until soft.

- Add peas, salt and pepper. Stir 1 minute.

- Add lemon juice and thyme.

- Spoon peas into squash cups.

- Bake uncovered 6 – 8 minutes.

6 SERVINGS

Butternut Squash Soufflé

4 teaspoons butter

2 cups hot puréed butternut squash

¼ cup milk, warmed

3 tablespoons butter

¼ cup finely chopped parsley

2 tablespoons chopped chives

1 teaspoon freshly grated gingerroot

½ teaspoon salt

3 large eggs, separated

¼ teaspoon cream of tartar

- Preheat oven to 400°F.

- Butter a 6-cup soufflé dish with 4 teaspoons butter.

- In a large bowl, whisk together the squash, milk, 3 table-spoons butter, parsley, chives, ginger and salt. Add egg yolks and beat until mixture is blended.

- In another bowl, beat egg whites until foamy.

- Add cream of tartar and continue to beat until stiff.

- Gently stir about ⅓ of the whites into the squash mixture.

- Fold in the remaining whites.

- Turn into the prepared dish and place in oven.

- Immediately lower heat to 375°F. and bake 35 minutes until top is nicely browned and soufflé feels firm to the touch.

- Serve immediately.

4 SERVINGS

A stunning way to serve squash. It has a light texture and subtle taste.

To achieve the best results when making soufflés, be sure to have the eggs at room temperature.

Baked Wild Rice

The water chestnuts add a delicious crunch.

1 cup wild rice

½ pound mushrooms, sliced

3 tablespoons minced onion

½ cup water chestnuts, sliced

3 cups chicken broth

4 tablespoons butter

- Preheat oven to 325°F. Rinse rice thoroughly. Drain.
- Combine rice, mushrooms, onion and water chestnuts in a 2-quart heat-proof dish. Add chicken broth to dish and dot with butter.
- Cover dish and bake for 1½ hours. Check dish after 1 hour of baking and remove some liquid if necessary.

4 SERVINGS

Braised Tarragon Cherry Tomatoes

An easy but elegant way to serve cherry tomatoes.

24 to 30 cherry tomatoes (very small)

4 tablespoons clarified butter

1 teaspoon tarragon

1½ teaspoons granulated sugar

½ teaspoon salt

- Preheat oven to 350°F. Wash and pat dry tomatoes. Place in shallow baking dish.
- Mix together butter, tarragon, sugar and salt. Pour over tomatoes and gently coat.
- Bake 5 – 8 minutes, stirring occasionally until heated through. Do not let tomatoes become mushy.

6 SERVINGS

Quincy Market

Paul Revere House

Green Beans in Dill-Walnut Sauce

1½ pounds fresh green beans (small, whole are best but large, cut up will do)

¾ cup green onions

3 tablespoons fresh or 1 tablespoon dried parsley

4 tablespoons fresh or 1 tablespoon dried dill

3 tablespoons apple cider vinegar

¾ cup chopped walnuts

½ cup vegetable oil

Salt and freshly ground black pepper, to taste

GARNISH:

Dill sprigs

- Cook green beans for 8 minutes until just tender. Drain and rinse with cold water.

- In blender, combine green onions, parsley, dill, vinegar, walnuts and oil. Blend and add more oil if necessary.

- Season to taste with salt and pepper.

- Pour sauce over beans.

- Toss and chill beans for 1 – 2 hours.

- Bring to room temperature before serving.

- Garnish with sprigs of fresh dill.

6 – 8 SERVINGS

Note: If using dried dill instead of fresh, sprinkle the smaller amount directly over beans.

Always rub herbs, dried or fresh, briskly between your fingers to release the flavor oils.

A wonderful variation on the traditional bean salad.

Tomatoes Provencale

*Spicy and rich, a
flavorful way to serve
ripe tomatoes.*

6 firm red ripe tomatoes

Salt and freshly ground black pepper, to taste

2 pressed garlic cloves

3 tablespoons minced shallots or green onions

¼ cup fresh or 2 tablespoons dried minced basil

¼ cup fresh or 2 tablespoons dried minced parsley

Dash of thyme

¼ cup olive oil

½ cup fine dry bread crumbs made from French bread

- Preheat oven to 400°F.

- Juice and seed tomatoes. Sprinkle with salt and pepper and invert on paper towels for ½ hour.

- In a mixing bowl, toss together garlic, shallots, basil, parsley, thyme, salt, pepper, olive oil and bread crumbs.

- Fill tomatoes with the stuffing. Place filled tomatoes in a shallow, oiled pan just large enough to hold them in one layer.

- Bake for 10 – 15 minutes until tomatoes are tender but hold their shape and bread crumbs are nicely browned.

6 SERVINGS

Note: May be prepared several hours in advance of cooking.

Squash Grand Marnier

1 quart cooked and mashed butternut squash

3 tablespoons butter, melted

⅓ cup light brown sugar, firmly packed

½ teaspoon salt

Dash of freshly grated nutmeg

Dash of ground cinnamon

2 egg yolks, beaten

2 tablespoons Grand Marnier

½ cup chopped walnuts

2 egg whites, beaten to stiff peaks

- Preheat oven to 350°F.
- Combine squash, butter, sugar, salt, nutmeg, cinnamon, egg yolks, Grand Marnier and walnuts. Mix together well.
- Fold in beaten egg whites.
- Place mixture in 2-quart heat-proof dish.
- Bake 25 – 30 minutes.

6 – 8 SERVINGS

Note: May be prepared in advance up to adding egg whites.

The combination of spices give this squash a delightful flavor and aroma. A wonderful fall dish.

Carmelized Carrots

2 cups peeled, sliced carrots (⅛" thick), or tiny baby carrots, peeled

½ cup chicken or beef broth or bouillon

1 tablespoon butter

2 tablespoons honey

1 tablespoon light brown sugar

¼ teaspoon marjoram

- Cook carrots in broth until tender-crisp, approximately 10 minutes. Remove carrots from saucepan and keep warm. Reserve stock.
- Add butter, honey and sugar to stock in pan and boil for 2 minutes.
- Remove from heat. Add carrots and marjoram, stirring to coat. Serve immediately.

6 SERVINGS

The glaze enhances the earthy flavor of these sweet morsels.

Duchess Sweet Potatoes

A very pretty and tasty way to serve sweet potatoes. Perfect for an elegant dinner party or buffet.

1 pound sweet potatoes	**1 egg yolk**
½ pound baking potatoes	**Melted butter for drizzling over potatoes**
2 tablespoons butter	
1 egg	

- Preheat oven to 350°F. Butter a cookie sheet.
- Peel and boil sweet and baking potatoes until tender.
- Put potatoes through a food mill into a large bowl.
- Add 2 tablespoons butter, the egg and egg yolk, beating the mixture until smooth.
- Scoop potato mixture into a pastry bag fitted with a decorative tip and pipe rosettes onto prepared cookie sheet. (If mixture is too thick to pipe, thin with heavy cream.)
- Drizzle melted butter over the rosettes. Bake for 15 minutes.
- Increase heat to broil. Place rosettes 6″ from heat and cook for a few minutes to brown, watching carefully.

4 (8 ROSETTES) SERVINGS

Note: *The rosettes may be prepared up to baking, then refrigerated. To serve, bake rosettes for 30 minutes in preheated oven, then finish in broiler.*

Broccoli Dijon

The tangy mustard sauce adds a new dimension to staid broccoli.

1 bunch of broccoli, washed, cut up	**1 tablespoon red wine vinegar**
2 tablespoons butter	**2 tablespoons olive oil**
1½ teaspoons Worcestershire sauce	**Pinch of cayenne pepper**
1 teaspoon Dijon mustard	**Salt and freshly ground black pepper, to taste**

- Steam broccoli or stir fry in hot oil until tender.
- In a small saucepan, combine butter, Worcestershire sauce, mustard, vinegar, oil and cayenne. Stirring constantly, heat sauce to a boil. Adjust seasoning.
- Pour sauce over hot broccoli and serve immediately.

8 SERVINGS

Cheddar Potatoes

12 medium potatoes, washed and unpeeled

⅔ cup chopped green onion

1 teaspoon salt

1 teaspoon freshly ground black pepper

3 cups sour cream

4 cups grated Cheddar cheese

1 stick butter

- Preheat oven to 350°F.

- In 6-quart covered saucepan, boil potatoes for approximately 30 minutes or until fork-tender.

- Drain and cool for 15 minutes.

- Peel and cube cooked potatoes. Place in a 3-quart heat-proof dish or 9″ × 13″ roasting pan.

- Add chopped green onion and toss lightly.

- In a small bowl, stir salt and pepper into sour cream. Set aside.

- In a 3-quart saucepan over low heat, combine cheese and butter, stirring constantly until melted. Mixture will be thick.

- Remove from heat.

- Add sour cream to cheese mixture and pour over potatoes and onion. Toss lightly.

- Bake uncovered for 40 minutes.

10 SERVINGS

Note: *Potatoes may be prepared early in day and placed in refrigerator covered. Bring to room temperature before baking.*

Hearty and cheesy, these potatoes compliment any full-bodied entree.

Squash Gratin

Swiss cheese and squash, a delightful combination of flavors. Perfect with turkey.

8 cups winter squash cut into ½″ cubes

1 teaspoon grated fresh ginger

2 large garlic cloves, minced

4 tablespoons butter

6 tablespoons all purpose flour

4 cups milk

Salt and freshly ground black pepper, to taste

6 tablespoons fresh white bread crumbs

6 tablespoons grated Swiss cheese

- Preheat oven to 325°F.
- Steam the squash, ginger and garlic in a steaming basket over 1 inch of water for 10 minutes. The squash should not be completely cooked.
- Remove the basket and squash mixture and boil down the water until ½ cup remains.
- In a 4-quart pan, melt butter, and blend in the flour. Cook until bubbly, about 2 minutes. Do not let it color. Remove from heat.
- Add reduced liquid when bubbling stops, whisking in well.
- Whisk in the milk. Return to the heat and simmer 2 minutes.
- Season to taste with salt and pepper.
- Stir in the steamed squash mixture and pour all in a large buttered baking dish.
- Top with crumbs and cheese.
- Bake for 1½ hours.

8 – 10 SERVINGS

Note: May be prepared one day ahead up to baking. Bring to room temperature before baking.

Elegant Wild Rice with Mushrooms and Almonds

1 cup wild rice

Boiling water

1 pound fresh mushrooms, sliced

1 medium onion, chopped

6 tablespoons butter, divided

2 teaspoons salt

¼ teaspoon freshly ground black pepper

½ cup sliced almonds

3 cups chicken broth

1½ cups heavy cream

6 tablespoons freshly grated Parmesan cheese, divided

A rich and unusual way to prepare wild rice. The almonds and cheese add a wonderful flavor.

- Preheat oven to 350°F. Grease heat-proof dish.

- Wash rice and cover with boiling water. Soak 1 hour, drain well.

- Sauté mushrooms and onion in 1 tablespoon butter for 10 minutes.

- Melt remaining butter.

- In prepared dish, combine rice, mushrooms, onion, melted butter, salt, pepper, almonds, chicken broth, cream and 3 tablespoons Parmesan. Toss lightly.

- Bake covered for 1½ hours. Remove from oven.

- Increase oven heat to 450°F.

- Sprinkle with remaining Parmesan cheese.

- Bake uncovered 5 minutes longer.

6 SERVINGS

Note: *May add 3 cups of cooked, cubed chicken to make this an entrée.*

May be prepared in advance up to baking. May be frozen. Defrost before baking.

Mushrooms Au Gratin

Very rich and luscious. A little goes a long way!

4 tablespoons butter

1 pound fresh mushrooms, halved

1 tablespoon shallots, minced

Salt and freshly ground black pepper, to taste

1 cup whipping cream

6 ounces Gruyère cheese, shredded

- Preheat oven to 350°F.
- In a large skillet, melt butter and add mushrooms, shallots, salt and pepper. Sauté over medium heat for 3 – 5 minutes or until golden. Pour off liquid.
- Pour cream over mushrooms and let simmer for 10 minutes or until liquid is reduced by half.
- Remove mushroom mixture to small gratin dish. Sprinkle cheese over top of mushroom mixture.
- Bake for 20 minutes or until bubbly.

4 – 6 SERVINGS

Boston Bourbon Sweet Potatoes

Delicious! A wonderful accompaniment to turkey or ham. The combination of bourbon and maple syrup make these potatoes extra special.

½ cup unsalted butter, melted

⅓ cup brown sugar

¼ cup bourbon

¼ cup maple syrup

2 pounds fresh sweet potatoes*, peeled, sliced ⅛″ thick

- Preheat oven to 400°F. Grease two round glass or ceramic pie dishes or one large heat-proof dish.
- Mix together butter, sugar, bourbon and maple syrup in 2-cup measuring cup.
- Overlap sweet potato slices in layers in prepared dishes. Pour butter-sugar mixture over sweet potatoes.
- Bake for 45 minutes until potatoes are soft.
- Serve cut into wedges. Drizzle maple syrup on top to garnish.

8 SERVINGS

* Yams may be used in place of sweet potatoes.

Note: If sweet potatoes begin to get too brown, cover with foil during last 15 – 20 minutes of baking.

Orange Scented Rice

½ cup minced celery, using leaves as well

2 tablespoons minced onion

4 tablespoons butter

1 tablespoon grated fresh or 1 teaspoon dried orange rind

1 teaspoon salt

⅛ teaspoon thyme

1 cup freshly squeezed orange juice

1½ cups water

1 cup rice

One 1″ cinnamon stick

- In medium saucepan, sauté celery and onion in butter.

- Add orange peel, salt, thyme, orange juice and water and bring to boil.

- Add rice and cinnamon stick. Cover and simmer 15 – 20 minutes until rice is done.

- Fluff rice with fork and remove cinnamon stick.

6 SERVINGS

An aromatic way of cooking rice. A perfect accompaniment to fish, chicken or pork.

Add toasted sesame seeds to garnish for crunch.

Spinach Cheese Tart

Spinach has a water content of 80 – 90 percent. It is very perishable and will wilt easily.

Wash just prior to using or the leaves may rot from any water left on them.

3 tablespoons minced scallion

3 tablespoons butter, divided

1½ cups spinach cooked, drained and chopped

¼ teaspoon freshly grated nutmeg

¼ teaspoon salt

¼ teaspoon freshly grated black pepper

4 ounces cream cheese, softened

4 ounces Bucheron cheese (French goat cheese)

4 eggs, separated

½ cup heavy cream

Pinch of salt

⅓ cup fresh bread crumbs

1 pie crust, ⅛″ thick, in 9″ flan pan with removeable fluted rim, baked until golden brown.

- Preheat oven to 375°F.

- In a large skillet sauté scallion in 2 tablespoons butter over medium heat until soft.

- Add spinach, nutmeg, salt and pepper and cook 5 minutes, stirring constantly.

- Transfer the spinach mixture to a large bowl and add the cream cheese and Bucheron cheese. Blend well.

- Add the egg yolks one at a time, mixing well. Add the heavy cream, mixing well.

- In a large bowl beat the egg whites with a pinch of salt until stiff peaks are formed. Fold into spinach mixture.

- Pour the spinach mixture into the prepared crust and dot the top with the remaining 1 tablespoon of butter. Sprinkle top with bread crumbs.

- Bake in the middle of the oven for 25 minutes until puffed and browned.

- Remove tart from pan and transfer to a rack to cool. Serve cut into wedges.

12 SERVINGS

Quincy Market

Next to Boston's Faneuil Hall on State Street is the bustling marketplace known as Quincy Market. The original market was the idea of Boston's mayor, Josiah Quincy, who wanted to increase and develop the city's market facilities. At that time, the area was unwanted and undeveloped land bordering Boston Harbor. The mayor ordered the land filled in to accommodate three structures: Quincy Market and the North and South Market buildings. Designed by the architect Alexander Parris, construction of the principal granite building, Quincy Market, was begun in 1825. With its two stories, Greek porticoes and domed pavilion, Quincy Market quickly became a central meeting place for those engaged in commerce.

The market was completely renovated in 1976. Today, all types of food emporia, restaurants, fine clothing stores, shops and other businesses are housed in the three buildings. Every Friday and Saturday, throughout the year, farmers set up their fresh fruit, vegetable and fish stands in Haymarket, just around the corner. In the summertime, the area is a favorite stop for tourists of all nationalities and a natural stage for the many street performers of the city.

Beacon Hill Chocolate Velvet

To make shaved chocolate curls, let semi-sweet chocolate squares stand in a warm place (90 – 100°F.) for 5 – 10 minutes.

Using a vegetable peeler scrape from the bottom and sides of the square using long strokes.

Homemade or purchased sponge or chocolate cake, thinly sliced

3 egg yolks

2 tablespoons Crème de Cocoa

2 tablespoons rum

1 tablespoon instant coffee granules

1 pound semi-sweet chocolate

5⅓ tablespoons butter

½ cup confectioners' sugar

2 pints heavy cream, divided

3 egg whites, stiffly beaten

GARNISH:

Semi-sweet chocolate shavings

- Line a round 3 – 4 quart bowl with plastic wrap.

- Line bowl with a thin layer of cake.

- Mix the egg yolks, Crème de Cocoa, rum and coffee granules together.

- Melt the chocolate and butter over simmering water .

- Remove chocolate mixture from heat and stir in confectioners' sugar. Cool.

- Stir chocolate mixture into egg yolk mixture.

- Whip 1 pint heavy cream and fold into the stiffly beaten egg whites.

- Fold egg whites into first egg yolk-chocolate mixture.

- Fill prepared cake-lined bowl with chocolate mixture and chill until well set or overnight.

- Whip second pint of heavy cream. Sweeten to taste.

- Turn cake upside down, remove plastic wrap and cover entire surface with whipped cream. Sprinkle with chocolate shavings.

- Refrigerate until ready to serve.

10 – 12 SERVINGS

Note: May make cake 1 – 2 days ahead, then cover with whipped cream the day of serving.

Mocha Chocolate Chip Cookies

3 cups semi-sweet chocolate chips, divided

1 stick butter

4 ounces unsweetened chocolate

½ cup all purpose flour

½ teaspoon baking powder

½ teaspoon salt

4 eggs, room temperature

1½ cups granulated sugar

1½ tablespoons instant coffee granules

2 teaspoons vanilla extract

- Preheat oven to 350°F. Line cookie sheets with parchment paper or wax paper.*

- Melt 1½ cups chocolate chips, butter and unsweetened chocolate over simmering water.

- Stir mixture until smooth, then remove from heat.

- Combine flour, baking powder and salt.

- With electric mixer, beat together eggs, sugar, coffee granules and vanilla until mixed.

- Stir in cooled chocolate mixture, then flour.

- Add remaining 1½ cups chocolate chips.

- Drop batter onto prepared sheets by teaspoonfuls.

- Bake until cookies are crackled and shiny outside but still soft inside, about 8 minutes.

- Cool for 15 minutes before removing from parchment.

- Store in covered container.

7 DOZEN

* Note: Do not reuse parchment paper.

Chocolate and cocoa are both derived from a bean of an evergreen tree.

Chocolate liquor is extracted from the hulled beans and molded into solid bars.

Mousse Cake with Raspberries

The best sweet chocolate is made by combining the melted bitter or baking chocolate with 35% cocoa butter and finely milled sugar and flavorings.

1 pound dark sweet chocolate

1 stick plus 2 tablespoons butter

4 large eggs, room temperature, divided

1 tablespoon granulated sugar

1 tablespoon vanilla extract

1 tablespoon all purpose flour

1 cup fresh or frozen raspberries, puréed in blender and sieved to remove seeds

2 cups heavy cream, whipped

- Preheat oven to 425°F.
- Butter and flour an 8″ round of wax paper to fit bottom of a buttered 8″ round cake pan.
- Melt chocolate with butter in top of double boiler over very low heat.
- Beat eggs and sugar at high speed with mixer for 10 minutes or until tripled in volume.
- Add vanilla while beating.
- Sift flour over top of egg mixture and fold in gently.
- Fold ⅓ of this mixture into chocolate to lighten it, then fold chocolate back into the remaining eggs.
- Pour into cake pan and bake for no more than 15 minutes. Cake will be soft in the center.
- Cool and place in freezer at least overnight. Remove 1 hour before serving.
- Spread puréed raspberries over top and decorate with whipped cream. Serve with extra whipped cream on side.

12 SERVINGS

Brahmin Brownies

2 eggs

1 cup granulated sugar

2 ounces unsweetened chocolate

1 stick butter or margarine

1 teaspoon vanilla extract

½ cup sifted all purpose flour

⅛ teaspoon salt

¾ cup chopped pecans or walnuts

- Preheat oven to 350°F. Grease an 8″ × 8″ × 2″ baking pan.

- In a small bowl, beat eggs with electric mixer, gradually beating in sugar until mixture is light and fluffy.

- In a small saucepan, melt chocolate and butter over low heat. Cool slightly.

- Gently stir in chocolate mixture and vanilla.

- Fold in flour and salt until well blended.

- Stir in nuts.

- Pour into prepared pan.

- Bake for 30 minutes or until shiny and firm on top.

- Cool in pan on wire rack before cutting.

16 SQUARES

The first known use of cocoa beans was by the Aztecs. They made a drink from the beans called "Cacahautl" or "gift from the gods".

Cortez brought the chocolate back to Spain and eventually it was introduced throughout Europe.

Chocolate Glacé Marengo

CRUST:

36 chocolate wafers, crushed

6 tablespoons butter, melted

OR

18 Oreo cookies, crushed

3 tablespoons butter, melted

FILLING:

8 egg whites, room temperature

2 pinches salt

2 pinches cream of tartar

½ cup granulated sugar

4 cups whipping cream

2 tablespoons vanilla extract

2 packages (12 ounces each) semi-sweet chocolate chips

1 cup slivered almonds, toasted at 325°F. for 5 minutes

SAUCE:

12 ounces good quality milk chocolate (type with hazelnuts is nice)

1 cup half and half

- Preheat oven to 350°F.

- TO PREPARE THE CRUST: Mix together chocolate wafers and melted butter, or Oreos and butter.

- Press firmly into bottom of 10″ springform pan.

- Bake for 5 minutes, so crumbs do not fall apart.

- TO PREPARE THE FILLING: Beat egg whites until soft peaks form.

- Add salt and cream of tartar. Beat until stiff.

- Add sugar, 1 tablespoon at a time, and beat until very stiff peaks form.

- Transfer mixture to a large bowl, preferably metal, that can be put in the freezer.

Continued on next page

- In the same bowl that egg whites were beaten in, beat cream and vanilla until stiff. Fold in egg whites.

- Place bowl in freezer until ice crystals form, approximately 1 hour.

- In heavy saucepan, over low heat melt chocolate chips and stir in toasted almonds.

- While mixture is hot, fold it into the cold cream mixture. (Small chunks of chocolate slivers will form when the hot mixture hits the cold.)

- Pour mixture into crust and cover tightly with foil. Freeze.

- Remove from freezer 30 – 45 minutes before serving. Remove sides of springform pan and refrigerate.

- TO PREPARE THE SAUCE: In a heavy saucepan, melt milk chocolate over low heat with 2 tablespoons half-and-half.

- Stir in enough half and half to make desired consistency.

- Slice glacé and serve with warm sauce.

16 – 18 SERVINGS

Note: *Cake may be prepared ahead and frozen for months. Recipe may be halved.*

Fudge Rum Cake

Decorate this rich confection with fresh mint leaves and candied violets.

CAKE:

¾ cup plus 2 tablespoons all purpose flour

½ teaspoon baking powder

½ teaspoon salt

¼ teaspoon baking soda

2 ounces unsweetened chocolate

1¼ cups granulated sugar

1 tablespoon unsweetened cocoa powder

⅓ cup boiling water

1½ sticks unsalted butter, cut in pieces

2 large eggs

½ cup sour cream

1 tablespoon dark rum or bourbon

GLAZE:

3 ounces semi-sweet chocolate, broken in pieces

¼ cup sifted confectioners' sugar

2 tablespoons butter

2 tablespoons water

Pinch of salt

1 tablespoon rum or bourbon

- Preheat oven to 325°F. Butter bottom and flour sides of 10″ springform pan. Line bottom with wax paper. Butter paper.
- TO PREPARE THE CAKE: Combine flour, baking powder, salt and baking soda in food processor. Process 5 seconds. Transfer mixture to wax paper.
- Combine chocolate, sugar and cocoa in processor. Process 1 minute.
- With motor running, add boiling water. Add butter. Process 1 minute. Add eggs. Process 1 minute.
- Scrape sides of bowl. Then add sour cream and rum. Process 5 seconds.
- Add flour mixture. Process using only 4 to 5 on-off motions, just until the mixture shows no white. Do not overprocess or batter will be too thin.
- Bake in middle of oven until cake pulls away from pan, approximately 50 minutes.
- Remove cake from oven. Cool completely.
- Remove sides, invert cake and lift off paper.
- TO PREPARE THE GLAZE: Combine chocolate, sugar, butter, water and salt over simmering water until chocolate is melted. Remove and stir in rum. Refrigerate 15 – 20 minutes.
- Pour glaze over cake, spreading evenly.

10 – 12 SERVINGS

Light Sweet Chocolate Mousse

8 ounces sweet chocolate

6 eggs, separated

3 tablespoons water

¼ cup sweet liqueur, Amaretto or Grand Marnier

2 cups heavy cream

6 tablespoons granulated sugar

GARNISH:

Whipped cream

Grated chocolate

- Cut the chocolate into ½″ pieces and melt in the top of a double boiler over simmering water.

- Put the yolks in a heavy saucepan and add the water. Place the saucepan over very low heat while beating vigorously and constantly with a wire whisk.

- When the yolks start to thicken add the liqueur, beating constantly.

- Cook until the sauce reaches the consistency of hollandaise. Remove from heat.

- Add the melted chocolate to the sauce and fold it in. Scrape sauce into a mixing bowl.

- Beat the cream until stiff, adding 2 tablespoons of the sugar toward the end of the beating.

- Fold this mixture into the chocolate mixture.

- Beat the whites until soft peaks start to form. Beat in the remaining sugar and continue beating until stiff.

- Fold egg whites into mousse.

- Spoon mixture into a serving bowl.

- When ready to serve, garnish with whipped cream and grated chocolate.

12 SERVINGS

Chocolate leaves make an interesting decorative garnish and are surprisingly simple to do.

Melt 4 ounces of sweet or semi-sweet chocolate over very low heat.

Using a narrow spatula or brush spread the chocolate on the underside of an edible washed and dried leaf. (Dogwood, lemon or holly.)

Place on wax paper and chill until chocolate is firm, about 15 minutes.

Carefully peel leaves away from chocolate.

Chocolate Angel Pie

Do not attempt to make a meringue when the weather is humid. The slow baking process actually dries the meringue.

Humidity in the air will be absorbed back into the meringue after baking and cause it to collapse.

MERINGUE CRUST:

2 egg whites

⅛ teaspoon cream of tartar

⅛ teaspoon salt

½ cup super fine granulated sugar

½ cup chopped pecans

½ teaspoon vanilla extract

FILLING:

¾ cup milk

1 small package (6 ounces) semi-sweet chocolate, in small pieces

1 teaspoon instant espresso coffee

Pinch of salt

3 egg yolks

½ teaspoon vanilla extract

1 cup heavy cream

½ cup chopped pecans

GARNISH:

Grated chocolate

- Preheat oven to 275°F. Butter an 8" pie pan.
- TO PREPARE THE MERINGUE: Beat egg whites, cream of tartar and salt until soft peaks form, gradually adding sugar until peaks are shiny and stiff.
- Fold in pecans and vanilla and spread into prepared pan, building up around the sides.
- Bake for 45 minutes, turn off heat and leave crust in oven and the door ajar for 1 hour. Remove crust and chill.
- TO PREPARE THE FILLING: Scald milk in heavy saucepan over moderate heat. Add the chocolate, espresso and a pinch of salt and whisk the mixture until the chocolate and coffee are melted and dissolved.
- Remove the pan from heat and add the egg yolks, one at a time, beating well after each addition. Cook the mixture over moderately low heat for 1 – 2 minutes or until it thickens.
- Transfer mixture to a large bowl, stir in vanilla and let it cool.
- In a chilled bowl, beat cream until it holds stiff peaks and fold into the chocolate mixture.
- Spoon half the filling into the shell. Sprinkle the pecans on top, then add the remaining filling.
- Chill the pie loosely covered for 2 hours. Garnish with grated chocolate.

1 PIE

Chocolate Coronet

18 ladyfingers, split

½ cup freshly squeezed
   orange juice

2 packages (8 ounces each)
   cream cheese,
   room temperature

½ teaspoon salt

¾ cup granulated sugar

2 teaspoons vanilla extract

3 eggs, separated

12 ounces sweet German
   cooking chocolate, melted
   and cooled to room
   temperature

2 cups heavy cream, whipped

½ cup semi-sweet chocolate
   chips, melted and cooled

3 tablespoons water

Confectioners' sugar

*In America, chocolate
was a special treat and
had to be imported until a
mill was started in
Dorchester,
Massachusetts in 1765.
The price went down and
chocolate became a very
popular drink.*

*The popularity increased
even more so after the
Boston Tea Party in 1773,
when Colonists started
boycotting tea.*

- Arrange ladyfingers rounded (outside) sides up, close together, on cookie sheet or wax paper and sprinkle with or spoon on juice. Do not soak them.

- Arrange ladyfingers around inside rim of 9″ springform pan (3″ high) and put remaining pieces on bottom.

- In a large bowl, combine cream cheese, salt, sugar and vanilla and beat until smooth.

- Add egg yolks and beat until smooth.

- Blend in cooled sweet chocolate.

- In separate bowl, beat egg whites until stiff and fold into the cheese-chocolate mixture along with the whipped cream.

- Pour into the springform pan and chill overnight.

- Before serving, melt chocolate in double boiler and mix in water, stirring until smooth.

- Remove rim of pan.

- Pour chocolate mixture on top and spread lightly, using a metal spatula.

- Brush ladyfingers with confectioners' sugar.

10 – 12 SERVINGS

Chocolate Pound Cake

When baking chocolate brownies and cakes, dust the baking pan with a mixture of unsweetened cocoa and flour.

1 cup cocoa powder

2 cups sifted all purpose flour

½ teaspoon baking powder

1 teaspoon salt

2 tablespoons instant coffee granules

3 sticks unsalted butter

3 cups granulated sugar

2 teaspoons vanilla extract

5 eggs

1 cup buttermilk

¼ cup water

- Preheat oven to 325°F. Butter and flour a 10″ tube pan.

- Sift together cocoa, flour, baking powder, salt and coffee. Set aside.

- In a large bowl, cream butter with an electric mixer until light and fluffy. While beating, add sugar in a slow stream, beating for 5 minutes at high speed.

- Slow speed and add vanilla. Add eggs, one at a time, beating briefly after each addition.

- Mix together buttermilk and water.

- Mix dry ingredients and buttermilk into butter mixture, starting and ending with dry ingredients.

- Pour well-blended mixture into prepared pan and bake in upper third of oven for 1 hour and 20 minutes or until knife inserted in center comes out clean.

- Let cake rest in pan 20 minutes before removing. Cool completely on a cake rack before serving.

10 SERVINGS

DESSERTS

Paul Revere House

In the North End is Paul Revere's house, the oldest structure in Boston, at 19 North Square. Built after Boston's Great Fire of 1676, the house was a hundred years old when Paul Revere and his family moved into it. Revere paid just over 214 Pounds with a 160 Pound mortgage for the two-story house, which he soon expanded to three floors. Here, Revere, his wife and their sixteen children (from two marriages) lived from 1770 to 1800.

A multi-talented man, Paul Revere is best known for his midnight ride on April 19, 1775, to warn the Minutemen of the approach of the British Army. He was also an accomplished silversmith, dentist, designer, engraver and printer of paper money, the owner of a bell-foundry (he produced over four hundred bells for New England churches), and coppersmith (his firm was involved with copperplating the new State House dome and installing copper and brasswork on the U.S.S. Constitution). He was also an ardent rebel organizer and member of the Sons of Liberty. We celebrate the rich legacy of Paul Revere every Patriot's Day in Boston, on April 19.

Pumpkin and Cream Cheese Roll

The custom of carving faces into pumpkins probably began as a way to scare off the spirits celebrated on November 1, the day of the Dead. In Scotland they carve jack-o'-lanterns out of turnips.

CAKE:

¾ cup all purpose flour

1 teaspoon baking powder

2 teaspoons ground cinnamon

1 teaspoon pumpkin pie spice

½ teaspoon freshly grated nutmeg

½ teaspoon salt

3 eggs, beaten

1 cup granulated sugar

⅔ cup canned pumpkin purée

1 cup chopped walnuts

FILLING:

1 cup sifted confectioners' sugar

1 package (8 ounces) cream cheese, softened

6 tablespoons butter

1 teaspoon vanilla extract

- Preheat oven to 375°F. Grease a 15″ × 10″ × 1″ jelly roll pan and line with wax paper. Grease and flour wax paper.

- TO PREPARE THE CAKE: Sift flour, baking powder, cinnamon, pumpkin pie spice, nutmeg and salt together.

- In a large bowl, beat eggs and sugar until thick and fluffy.

- Beat pumpkin purée into egg mixture.

- Stir flour mixture all at once into egg mixture.

- Pour batter into prepared pan. Spread evenly.

- Sprinkle batter with nuts.

- Bake for 15 minutes until center springs back.

- Loosen cake with knife and invert onto a clean tea towel, sprinkled with confectioners' sugar.

- Pull off wax paper.

- Trim ¼″ from all sides.

Continued on next page

- From short side, roll up cake and towel together while warm.

- Place seam side down and cool completely.

- TO PREPARE THE FILLING: In a small bowl, beat together sugar, cream cheese, butter and vanilla until smooth.

- Unroll cake and spread evenly with cream cheese filling.

- Reroll cake and refrigerate at least 2 hours until ready to serve.

10 SERVINGS

Glazed Lemon Almond Pound Cake

CAKE:

1 cup blanched almonds

1 cup granulated sugar

2 sticks unsalted butter, softened

4 eggs

1 tablespoon freshly grated lemon rind

1 cup all purpose flour

1 teaspoon baking powder

¼ teaspoon salt

¼ cup fresh lemon juice

GLAZE:

¼ cup fresh lemon juice

2 cups confectioners' sugar

GARNISH:

Candied lemon slices

Candied violets

- Preheat oven to 350°F. Butter and flour 9" or 10" springform pan and line with buttered wax paper.

- TO PREPARE THE CAKE: In a food processor, grind the almonds finely with the sugar.

- In a large bowl, cream the butter and add the almond mixture. Beat the mixture with an electric mixer until it is light and fluffy.

- Add the eggs, one at a time, beating well after each addition.

- Beat in the rind.

- In another bowl, sift together the flour, baking powder and salt.

- Add flour mixture to the butter mixture alternately with the lemon juice, beginning and ending with the flour mixture. Stir well after each addition.

Continued on next page

- Pour the batter into prepared pan.

- Bake the cake in the middle of the oven for 40 minutes or until cake tester comes out clean.

- Let the cake cool for 5 minutes, then release side of springform pan.

- Let the cake cool completely.

- TO PREPARE THE GLAZE: In a small bowl, add the lemon juice. Gradually, sift the sugar over the juice, whisking the mixture until smooth.

- Pour the glaze over the top of the cake and gently smooth the top with a spatula, letting some of the glaze drip down the side.

- Garnish with candied lemon slices or candied violets.

10 – 12 SERVINGS

Note: *The cake may be made three days in advance and kept covered and chilled.*

Bavarian Apple Torte

A simple but elegant dessert to make when apples are in abundance.

CRUST:

1 stick butter or margarine, softened

⅓ cup granulated sugar

¼ teaspoon vanilla extract

1 cup sifted all purpose flour

FILLING:

1 package (8 ounces) cream cheese, softened

¼ cup granulated sugar

1 egg, slightly beaten

½ teaspoon vanilla extract

4 cups thinly sliced apples

½ teaspoon ground cinnamon

⅓ cup granulated sugar

¼ cup sliced almonds

- Preheat oven to 450°F.

- TO PREPARE THE CRUST: With a mixer beat butter, sugar and vanilla until well blended.

- Slowly stir in flour until mixture forms a soft dough.

- Press dough into bottom and 1½″ up sides of ungreased 9″ springform pan.

- TO PREPARE THE FILLING: Beat cream cheese and ¼ cup sugar until fluffy.

- Add egg and vanilla to cream cheese, beating until smooth.

- Pour cream cheese mixture over crust.

- Combine apples, cinnamon and ⅓ cup sugar. Layer over cream cheese mixture, decoratively.

- Sprinkle almonds on top.

- Bake for 10 minutes.

- Lower heat to 400°F. and bake for an additional 25 minutes.

- Cool on cake rack before removing sides of springform pan.

- Serve chilled or at room temperature.

8 – 10 SERVINGS

Blueberries in Cointreau

2 cups fresh blueberries, washed

2 tablespoons light brown sugar

½ teaspoon grated orange rind

3 tablespoons Cointreau

¼ cup heavy cream, whipped

- Place blueberries in a shallow mixing bowl.
- Sprinkle berries with brown sugar and orange rind and toss well to coat.
- Pour the Cointreau over berries and toss again.
- Cover berries with plastic wrap and refrigerate.
- Serve with whipped cream.

4 SERVINGS

Note: Cream should be whipped just before serving.

Store ripe berries in the refrigerator covered and unwashed until ready to use.

Massachusetts Maple Walnut Pie

3 eggs, beaten slightly

1 cup maple syrup (no substitutes)

2 tablespoons butter, melted

1 teaspoon vanilla extract

⅛ teaspoon salt

1 cup chopped walnuts

1 8″ pie crust, unbaked

- Preheat oven to 350°F.
- In medium bowl, beat together syrup, butter, vanilla and salt. Add eggs and nuts.
- Pour into crust and bake for 45 minutes or until knife inserted comes out clean.

1 PIE

Colonists learned about maple syrup from the Indians. They would put the sap in hollowed out logs with hot stones which would boil down the sap to syrup.

Another method of making the sap into syrup was to leave it out overnight to freeze and in the morning take off the layer of ice and use the syrup that had remained.

Pumpkin Cheesecake

In the supermarket or at a roadside stand, look for a pumpkin with a bright orange color and a blemish-free rind. It should feel heavy for its size.

½ cup gingersnap crumbs

4 packages (8 ounces each) cream cheese, softened

1½ cups granulated sugar

⅓ cup all purpose flour

2 teaspoons ground cinnamon

1 teaspoon freshly grated nutmeg

1 teaspoon ground cloves

¼ teaspoon ground allspice

Salt, to taste

6 eggs, room temperature

1 teaspoon vanilla extract

2 cups pumpkin purée

GARNISH:

Orange peel

Whipped cream

Candied ginger, chopped

- Preheat oven to 325°F. Butter well bottom and sides of 9″ springform pan.

- Sprinkle gingersnap crumbs on bottom and sides of pan. Chill until ready to fill.

- TO PREPARE THE FILLING: Beat cream cheese until fluffy.

- Add sugar, flour, cinnamon, nutmeg, cloves, allspice and salt to cream cheese. Beat to combine.

- Add eggs, one at a time, beating well after each addition.

- Add vanilla, beat well.

- Fold pumpkin purée into cream cheese mixture.

- Pour mixture into prepared pan.

- Bake for 1½ hours in middle of oven.

- Turn off oven, open door, and let cake stand in oven for 30 minutes.

- Cool cake. Cover loosely and chill overnight.

- Remove sides of springform pan.

- Garnish with orange peel, whipped cream and candied ginger.

10 SERVINGS

Non-Puritan Pears with Sherry Cream

A light elegant dessert after a filling meal.

½ **cup granulated sugar**

1 **cup water**

1 **drop red food coloring**

¼ **cup plus 2 tablespoons dry sherry, divided**

6 **Anjou pears, peeled, halved and cored**

4 **egg yolks**

⅛ **teaspoon salt**

1 **cup sifted confectioners' sugar**

1 **cup heavy cream, well chilled**

GARNISH:

Grated chocolate

- In medium saucepan, combine sugar, water and food coloring.

- Boil mixture over medium heat, stirring constantly. Boil syrup for 1 minute.

- Add 2 tablespoons sherry and pears to sugar mixture.

- Poach pears, covered, over low heat for 10 – 15 minutes, turning them several times.

- Cool pears in syrup mixture for 1 hour at room temperature, loosely covered.

- TO PREPARE THE SHERRY CREAM: In top of double boiler, beat egg yolks, salt and confectioners' sugar until mixture is combined well.

- Add ¼ cup sherry to egg yolk mixture.

- Cook egg mixture over simmering water for 5 – 7 minutes or until thickened, stirring occasionally.

- In chilled bowl, whip cream until it holds stiff peaks.

- Gently fold whipped cream into egg yolk mixture.

- Drain pears well and arrange in individual dessert bowls.

- Top pears with sauce.

- Garnish with grated chocolate.

6 SERVINGS

Indian Pudding with Hard Sauce

This classic New England dish derives its name from the use of corn or Indian corn, as the Colonists called it.

It is not a dish native to the Indians, as they did not have the necessary ingredients available to them.

3 cups milk

3 tablespoons yellow corn meal

½ cup dark molasses

1 egg

½ cup granulated sugar

1 tablespoon butter, melted

½ teaspoon ground ginger

½ teaspoon ground cinnamon

¼ teaspoon salt

- Preheat oven to 300°F. Grease a 2-quart heat-proof dish.
- In a medium saucepan, bring the milk to a boil.
- Gradually stir in corn meal with a wire whisk. Cook, stirring constantly until slightly thickened.
- Stir in molasses and remove from heat.
- In a large bowl, beat the egg. Add sugar, butter, ginger, cinnamon and salt.
- Pour hot mixture into spice mixture, whisking rapidly until well blended.
- Pour mixture into prepared dish.
- Bake 1 hour or until knife inserted in center comes out clean.
- Serve immediately.
- Top with hard sauce, whipped cream or ice cream.

6 SERVINGS

HARD SAUCE:

2 sticks unsalted butter, softened

1 cup confectioners' sugar

¼ cup brandy, rum or sherry

Freshly grated nutmeg, to taste

- In a medium bowl, cream butter and sugar well.
- Add the brandy a few drops at a time and beat until fluffy.
- Sprinkle with nutmeg and chill.

2 CUPS

Old North Church

Copp's Hill Burial Ground

Hazlenut Fruit Tart

CRUST:

1½ sticks butter

½ cup granulated sugar

2 egg yolks

1 teaspoon vanilla extract

1¼ cups ground hazelnuts

1½ cups all purpose flour

FILLING:

1½ pints fresh raspberries or 1½ quarts strawberries

1 package unflavored gelatin

2 tablespoons Grand Marnier

1 jar (10 ounces) red currant jelly

- TO PREPARE THE CRUST: Combine butter and sugar until thoroughly mixed.

- Add yolks slowly while beating.

- Add vanilla.

- In food processor, combine hazelnuts and flour.

- Add butter mixture to hazelnut mixture just to combine. Do not overmix. The mixture will be soft.

- Using fingers, gently press dough evenly into 12" tart pan with removable bottom. Crust should be ½" thick. Do not overwork crust.

- Place tart crust in refrigerator for 2 hours.

- Preheat oven to 375°F.

- Bake for 20 – 25 minutes until lightly browned.

- Cool completely on wire rack.

- TO PREPARE THE FILLING: Fill tart crust with berries.

- Combine gelatin and Grand Marnier in small pan. Let sit for 1 minute.

- Add jelly and stir over low heat for 3 – 4 minutes, until mixture has liquid consistency.

- Remove from heat and cool.

- Spoon liquid mixture over berries.

- Refrigerate tart for 2 – 3 hours before serving.

10 – 12 SERVINGS

Hazelnuts provide the perfect backdrop for either raspberries or strawberries.

South End Sour Cream Pound Cake

Our favorite version of a very traditional cake.

CAKE:

2 sticks unsalted butter, room temperature

3 cups granulated sugar

3 cups all purpose flour

⅛ teaspoon salt

¼ teaspoon baking soda

6 eggs, room temperature, separated and divided as follows: 6 yolks, 4 whites, 2 whites (for icing)

1 cup sour cream

1 teaspoon vanilla extract

½ teaspoon almond extract

FROSTING:

2 cups granulated sugar

⅛ teaspoon salt

6 tablespoons water

5 tablespoons light corn syrup

- Preheat oven to 300°F. Butter and flour a 12-cup tube or bundt pan.

- TO PREPARE THE CAKE: In a large bowl, cream butter and gradually add sugar until smooth and lemon-colored.

- Sift together flour, salt and baking soda.

- Beat egg yolks well, until lemon-colored.

- Add yolks to butter-sugar mixture and beat well.

- Alternately add flour mixture and sour cream to egg mixture, beating well after each addition. Add vanilla and almond extracts.

- In a medium bowl, beat 4 egg whites until they form shiny peaks. Fold egg whites gently into batter.

- Pour batter into prepared pan. Bake for 1½ hours or until cake tester comes out clean.

- TO PREPARE THE FROSTING: In a heavy saucepan, combine sugar, salt, water and corn syrup. Boil until a small amount forms a soft ball when dropped in ice water, 225°F. on a candy thermometer.

- In a medium bowl, beat 2 egg whites until light and frothy.

- Slowly add hot ingredients to egg whites, whisking constantly until mixture is spreadable. Frost cake.

10 – 12 SERVINGS

Note: Taking time to cream sugar and butter completely and adding small amounts of flour mix and sour cream are well worth the effort. Making the cake should not be rushed.

Frozen Amaretto Soufflé

10 macaroon cookies (2″ diameter)

2 cups heavy cream

6 egg yolks

2 eggs

¾ cup granulated sugar

¼ cup Amaretto liqueur

GARNISH:

Sliced almonds

- Preheat oven to 350°F. Attach a 2½″ buttered foil collar to a 1-quart soufflé dish.

- Crumble macaroons on cookie sheet. Bake for 15 minutes, then cool.

- In a food processor, grind macaroon crumbs until consistency of bread crumbs.

- In large bowl, whip cream until it peaks. Set aside.

- In another large bowl, beat egg yolks and eggs with sugar and Amaretto at high speed until thick, about 5 – 10 minutes.

- Fold in whipped cream and ¾ cup macaroon crumbs. Reserve remainder for garnish.

- Pour mixture into prepared soufflé dish.

- Cover with foil and freeze for at least 4 – 6 hours.

- Remove soufflé from freezer and carefully remove foil and collar.

- Garnish with remaining macaroon crumbs and sliced almonds.

- Serve immediately.

8 SERVINGS

A light but rich dessert, sure to please almond lovers.

Rhubarb Crisp

Younger stalks of rhubarb work best in this recipe. Never cook the leaves as they are poisonous.

5 cups chopped rhubarb, ½" pieces

1 cup granulated sugar

¼ cup all purpose flour

½ teaspoon ground cinnamon

TOPPING:

1 cup flour

1 cup packed brown sugar

½ cup old fashioned or quick oats

1 stick butter or margarine, melted

- Preheat oven to 375°F. Grease a 9" × 9" baking pan.
- In a large bowl, combine rhubarb with sugar, flour and cinnamon. Toss well. Place mixture in prepared pan.
- TO PREPARE THE TOPPING: In a small bowl, mix together flour, brown sugar, oatmeal and butter. Stir well and sprinkle over rhubarb.
- Bake for 30 – 35 minutes until bubbly and browned. Cool for 30 minutes before serving.

6 – 8 SERVINGS

Pumpkin Pecan Pie

The early Colonists rated their brick ovens in terms of the number of pies they would hold. There were most commonly 10 pie and 20 pie ovens.

3 eggs, slightly beaten

1 cup fresh or canned pumpkin purée

1 cup granulated sugar

½ cup dark corn syrup

1 teaspoon vanilla extract

½ teaspoon ground cinnamon

¼ teaspoon salt

1 cup pecans, chopped

1 pie crust, unbaked

GARNISH:

1 cup whipped cream

- Preheat oven to 350°F.
- In a small mixing bowl combine eggs, pumpkin, sugar, corn syrup, vanilla, cinnamon and salt. Mix thoroughly. Add pecans.
- Pour mixture into unbaked pie crust.
- Bake for 40 minutes or until center of pie is firm. Garnish pie with whipped cream.

1 PIE

Fresh Lemon Soufflé

2 envelopes unflavored gelatin

½ cup water

6 eggs

1½ cups and 2 teaspoons granulated sugar

⅔ cup fresh lemon juice

1 tablespoon grated lemon rind

2 cups heavy cream, divided

1 teaspoon vanilla extract

1 tablespoon confectioners' sugar

- In a skillet sprinkle gelatin over water to soften. Let sit 5 minutes, then gently heat until gelatin dissolves. Remove from heat.

- In a large bowl, combine eggs and sugar. Beat on high speed until soft peaks form, about 7 – 8 minutes.

- In a separate bowl, combine lemon juice, rind and cooled gelatin. Add to egg and sugar mixture. Blend thoroughly.

- Place in freezer. Stir every 2 minutes until mixture thickens, about 6 – 8 minutes.

- Whip 1½ cups cream with vanilla.

- Fold whipped cream into thickened lemon mixture.

- Spoon into a large soufflé dish or individual dessert dishes.

- Refrigerate at least 2 – 3 hours.

- Just before serving, whip remaining ½ cup cream with confectioners' sugar and garnish soufflé.

12 SERVINGS

Eggs should be at room temperature before beating to obtain the best volume. This may be achieved by placing the bowl of eggs to be beaten in a larger bowl containing warm water and stirring until warm to the touch.

Charlestown Cheesecake

1 box zwieback crackers, crushed

¼ pound unsalted butter, melted

1½ cups granulated sugar, divided

3 packages (8 ounces each) cream cheese

4 eggs, room temperature

1 teaspoon vanilla extract

2 cups sour cream

GARNISH:

Fruit or preserves

- Preheat oven to 350°F.
- TO PREPARE THE CRUST: In medium bowl, combine crushed zwieback crackers and butter.
- Press mixture into bottom of 9″ springform pan until firmly packed. Chill.
- TO PREPARE THE FILLING: In a large bowl, cream 1 cup sugar and cream cheese.
- Add eggs, one at a time, until well mixed.
- Add vanilla. Beat until smooth and creamy.
- Pour cream cheese mixture into crust.
- Bake for 40 – 45 minutes. Remove cake from oven.
- TO PREPARE THE TOPPING: In a small bowl, beat sour cream and ½ cup sugar at high speed.
- Gently spoon topping on cheesecake. Do not pour.
- Return cheesecake to the oven and bake 5 minutes until set.
- Cool well before cutting.
- Serve plain or topped with fruit or preserves.

8 – 12 SERVINGS

Note: *Cheesecake may be prepared 1 day before serving. Graham crackers may be used instead of zwiebacks. It is very important that eggs be at room temperature and that oven door is not opened while cheesecake is baking.*

Summer Blueberry Pie

4¼ cups fresh blueberries, divided

½ cup granulated sugar

½ cup water

2 tablespoons cornstarch, dissolved in a small amount of cold water

2 tablespoons Cointreau

1 9″ pie crust, baked at 325°F. for 8 minutes, cooled

GARNISH:

Whipped cream or vanilla ice cream

- Wash, sort and dry blueberries.

- In medium saucepan, combine 1¼ cups blueberries, sugar and water.

- Bring berries slowly to a boil. Cook for 10 minutes until berries are soft and pop their skins.

- Force berry mixture through a sieve.

- Place strained berry mixture into same saucepan.

- Add cornstarch mixture to berry purée, and cook gently until purée is thickened.

- Remove mixture from heat. Add Cointreau and chill.

- Gently combine thickened, cooled purée with fresh berries.

- Pour berry mixture into baked pie crust and chill.

- Serve pie with whipped cream or vanilla ice cream.

1 PIE

This pie may be made with equally good results using wild or cultivated blueberries.

Spice Apple Cake with Sherry Cream Sauce

Apples have a history dating back to when the first colonists settled in North America. They brought apple seeds which were planted in 1629 by the people of the Massachusetts Bay Colony.

John Chapman, better known as "Johnny Appleseed" was born in Massachusetts and was responsible for the popularity of apples in America.

He traveled from New England in the early 1800's with an axe, hoe, and bags of apple seeds gathered from the remains of apple cider presses.

He planted orchards all the way to the Ohio River Valley.

CAKE:

3 cups all purpose flour, sifted	**2 cups granulated sugar**
1½ teaspoons baking soda	**3 cups peeled, cored and chopped apples**
½ teaspoon salt	**1 cup pecans or walnuts, chopped**
½ teaspoon freshly grated nutmeg	**1½ cups vegetable oil**
1 teaspoon ground cinnamon	**3 eggs**

SAUCE:

3 egg yolks	**2 tablespoons dry sherry**
6 tablespoons confectioners' sugar	**1 cup heavy cream**

- Preheat oven to 350°F. Butter and flour a 10" tube pan.

- TO PREPARE THE CAKE: Sift flour, baking soda, salt, nutmeg and cinnamon together into a large bowl.

- Add sugar to flour mixture.

- Stir in apples and nuts.

- In a small bowl, combine the oil and eggs. Add to apple batter. Blend gently but thoroughly.

- Pour batter into prepared pan.

- Bake 1¼ hours.

- Cool in pan 10 minutes. Turn out onto a cake rack and cool completely.

- TO PREPARE THE SAUCE: In a medium bowl, beat the egg yolks until very light.

- Stir in sugar and sherry.

- Whip the cream until stiff peaks form.

- Fold whipped cream into egg yolk mixture and refrigerate.

- Serve cake with chilled sherry cream sauce.

8 – 10 SERVINGS

Fresh Peach 'n Praline Pie

CRUST:

1 9" pie crust, unbaked

1 teaspoon all purpose flour

FILLING:

3 tablespoons all purpose flour

¼ cup granulated sugar

¼ teaspoon salt

¼ teaspoon freshly grated nutmeg

½ cup light corn syrup

3 eggs

3 cups peeled, cubed fresh peaches

1 stick butter, melted

TOPPING:

¼ cup all purpose flour

½ cup coarsely chopped pecans

¼ cup firmly packed light brown sugar

2 tablespoons butter, softened

- Preheat oven to 400°F.

- TO PREPARE THE CRUST: Sprinkle prepared crust with flour and set aside.

- TO PREPARE THE FILLING: In a large bowl, combine flour, sugar, salt, nutmeg, corn syrup and eggs. Beat at medium speed with mixer for 1 minute.

- Stir peaches and melted butter into filling by hand and pour into crust.

- TO PREPARE THE TOPPING: In a small bowl, combine flour, pecans, brown sugar and softened butter, mixing well with fingers until crumbly.

- Sprinkle topping evenly over pie and bake for 45 minutes or until knife inserted in center comes out clean.

- Cool on wire rack.

- Serve with whipped cream or vanilla ice cream.

1 PIE

A flavorful variation on traditional peach pie.

3 cups cubed peaches equals 3 – 4 medium peaches.

Winter Fruitcake with Brandy Buttercream Frosting, Brandy Sauce or Vanilla Sauce

Applesauce is the special touch to this moist, spicy fruitcake.

CAKE:

1 cup light brown sugar

1 cup granulated sugar

2 sticks butter, softened

2 eggs, beaten

2 cups applesauce

2 teaspoons baking soda

3½ cups all purpose flour

2 teaspoons ground cinnamon

1 teaspoon ground cloves

½ teaspoon freshly grated nutmeg

½ cup maraschino cherries, drained and cut up

1 can (8 ounces) pineapple tidbits, drained

2 cups raisins

1 cup chopped pitted dates

1 cup chopped walnuts

¼ cup brandy

BRANDY BUTTERCREAM FROSTING:

5⅓ tablespoons butter, softened

1 box (16 ounces) confectioners' sugar

2 tablespoons milk

2 tablespoons brandy

GARNISH:

Maraschino cherry halves

- Preheat oven to 325°F. Grease two 9″ × 5″ × 3″ loaf pans and line bottoms with greased wax paper.

- TO PREPARE THE CAKE: In a large bowl, cream together the sugars and butter. Stir in eggs.

- In medium saucepan, warm applesauce with baking soda.

- Combine applesauce mixture with butter-sugar mixture.

- Sift together flour, cinnamon, cloves and nutmeg. Blend flour mixture into batter.

- Lightly flour cherries, pineapple, raisins, dates and walnuts. Add to batter.

- Divide mixture between the prepared pans. Bake for 1½ hours, or until a cake tester inserted comes out clean. Immediately pour brandy over hot cakes.

Continued on next page

- Serve cake frosted or with Brandy Sauce or Vanilla Sauce.

- TO PREPARE THE FROSTING: In a large bowl, cream together butter and confectioners' sugar.

- Add milk and brandy to frosting until spreadable.

- Frost cake when cool. Decorate with cherry halves.

2 LOAF CAKES

BRANDY SAUCE:

½ cup granulated sugar	2 tablespoons butter
1 tablespoon all purpose flour	1 teaspoon vanilla extract
	1 tablespoon brandy
⅛ teaspoon salt	
1 cup boiling water	

- In a small bowl, combine sugar, flour and salt.

- Pour water over sugar mixture. Stir well.

- Add butter, vanilla and brandy. Beat until thick.

- Serve warm.

VANILLA SAUCE:

½ cup granulated sugar	1 cup boiling water
1 tablespoon cornstarch	2 tablespoons butter
⅛ teaspoon salt	1 teaspoon vanilla extract

- In a small saucepan, combine sugar, cornstarch and salt.

- Pour water over sugar mixture stirring constantly.

- Boil for 5 minutes, stirring constantly, until thickened.

- Remove from heat and add butter and vanilla. Stir well.

- Serve warm or chilled.

Ice Cream Yule Log

The perfect dessert for your holiday entertaining. Besides being elegant in appearance, it may be made well in advance and serves a large group.

CAKE:

1 cup all purpose flour

⅓ cup plus 3 tablespoons cocoa powder, divided

5 eggs

¾ teaspoon baking powder

¼ teaspoon salt

1 cup granulated sugar

2 teaspoons vanilla extract

1 pint vanilla ice cream, softened

1 pint green mint chip ice cream, softened

CHOCOLATE FROSTING:

3½ cups sifted confectioners' sugar

½ cup cocoa powder

4 tablespoons butter or margarine

¼ teaspoon salt

1½ teaspoons vanilla extract

¼ cup plus 2 tablespoons milk

GARNISH:

Holly

Red berries

- Preheat oven to 400°F. Grease 15″ × 10″ × 1″ jelly roll pan and line with wax paper. Grease and flour wax paper.

- TO PREPARE THE CAKE: In a large bowl, stir flour and ⅓ cup cocoa together. Set aside.

- In another large bowl, combine eggs, baking powder and salt. Beat at high speed until foamy.

- Gradually add sugar to egg mixture, beating until thick and lemon-colored.

- Gently fold flour mixture and vanilla into egg mixture.

- Spread batter evenly over prepared pan.

Continued on next page

- Bake for 10 – 12 minutes.

- Sift 3 tablespoons cocoa in a 15″ × 10″ rectangle on a clean linen tea towel.

- When cake is done, immediately loosen from sides of pan and turn onto cocoa on tea towel. Peel off wax paper.

- Starting at wide end, roll up cake and towel together.

- Cool on wire rack, seam side down, for 25 minutes.

- Unroll cake and remove towel.

- Starting at wide end of cake, spread vanilla ice cream over half of cake.

- Spread mint ice cream over other half.

- Gently roll cake back up and carefully place on pan.

- Freeze cake until ice cream is very firm.

- TO PREPARE THE FROSTING: In a large bowl, combine sugar, cocoa, butter, salt, vanilla and ¼ cup milk. Beat until smooth.

- Add remaining milk, if needed, 1 tablespoon at a time, to make frosting of spreadable consistency.

- Remove cake from freezer.

- Diagonally cut a 4″ piece of cake from one end of roll.

- Place roll on freezer-proof serving tray, such as silver, positioning cut edge of short piece against side of longer piece to resemble a tree branch.

- Spread chocolate frosting over cake roll.

- Score frosting with fork tines so it resembles tree bark.

- Garnish with holly and red berries.

- Freeze until serving time. Return any leftovers to freezer immediately.

12 – 15 SERVINGS

Note: May substitute pink mint chip or peppermint ice cream.

Pumpkin Angel Pie with Gingersnap Crust

CRUST:

1½ cups gingersnap crumbs

4 tablespoons butter, melted

FILLING:

¾ cup dark brown sugar

½ teaspoon ground ginger

1 package (1 tablespoon) unflavored gelatin

3 eggs, separated

½ teaspoon salt

¾ cup milk

1½ teaspoons ground cinnamon

1 can (15 ounces) or ½ can (28 ounces) pumpkin purée

¾ teaspoon freshly grated nutmeg

⅓ cup granulated sugar

GARNISH:

Whipped cream and ground cinnamon

- Preheat oven to 350°F.

- TO PREPARE THE CRUST: Combine crumbs and butter. Press mixture into a 9″ pie pan and bake for 10 minutes. Cool. Turn off oven.

- TO PREPARE THE FILLING: In medium saucepan, combine brown sugar, gelatin, salt, cinnamon, nutmeg and ginger. Stir well.

- In a medium saucepan, add 3 slightly beaten egg yolks and the milk. Heat over medium heat just until boiling, stirring constantly. Remove pan from heat.

- Add pumpkin purée to egg mixture and whisk well.

- Chill pumpkin mixture well until mounds can be formed, at least 2 hours.

- In medium bowl, beat together 3 egg whites and sugar until stiff peaks form. Gently fold egg whites into chilled pumpkin mixture.

- Place mixture in cooled pie crust. Refrigerate at least 2 hours before serving. Garnish with whipped cream and cinnamon.

1 PIE

Old North Church

"Listen, my children, and you shall hear
Of the midnight ride of Paul Revere,
On the eighteenth of April, in Seventy-five;
Hardly a man is now alive
Who remembers that famous day and year.

He said to his friend, "If the British march
By land or sea from the town to-night,
Hang a lantern aloft in the belfry arch
Of the North Church tower as a signal light,-
One, if by land, and two, if by sea;
And I on the opposite shore will be,
Ready to ride and spread the alarm
Through every Middlesex village and farm,
For the country folk to be up and to arm."

-The Landlord's Tale
Henry Wadsworth Longfellow, 1863

At the time of Paul Revere's midnight ride, Old North Church was the highest point on the Boston skyline. From Charlestown on the other shore, on the eve of April 18, 1775, Revere spotted the light of two lanterns hung in the steeple.

Old North Church is located on Salem Street in the North End. It was built in 1723 and is Boston's oldest church in use. The original name was Christ Church (the first Old North Church, built in 1650, was burned down in 1676). Designed in the fashion of London churches, the most striking features are the spire which towers 191 feet above the ground and the magnificent eight bells which still ring.

The steeple was felled in 1804 by a hurricane and was reconstructed from a Charles Bulfinch design, only to be blown over again by a 1954 hurricane. Today a copy of the original colonial steeple stands firm. Brought over from Gloucester, England, in 1844, the eight bells are considered "the best and sweetest in America." They range in weight from 620 pounds to 1,545 pounds.

Yankee Molasses Chip Cookies

Molasses is the remains of extracting sugar from sugar cane. It was obtained in trade from the West Indies. They felt it not worth the expense of shipping to Europe and thus became an important staple in the Colonists home.

1½ sticks margarine, softened

1 cup granulated sugar

1 egg

¼ cup molasses

2 cups all purpose flour

2 teaspoons baking soda

¼ teaspoon salt

1 teaspoon ground cinnamon

½ teaspoon ground cloves

¾ teaspoon ground ginger

8 ounces chocolate chips

- Preheat oven to 350°F. Lightly grease cookie sheets.
- In a large bowl, cream margarine and sugar.
- Add egg and molasses. Beat until smooth.
- In a separate large bowl, mix together flour, baking soda, salt, cinnamon, cloves and ginger.
- Beat flour mixture into sugar mixture.
- Fold chocolate chips into dough.
- Drop dough by rounded teaspoonfuls on prepared cookie sheets.
- Bake for 8 – 10 minutes, or until lightly browned.
- Remove and cool on wire racks.

4 DOZEN COOKIES

U.S.S. Constitution

Colonel William Prescott Statue and Bunker Hill Monument

Coconut Orange Squares

½ stick butter or margarine, softened

1 cup granulated sugar

1 egg

1 tablespoon grated orange rind

1 tablespoon milk

1 cup flaked coconut

⅔ cup sifted all purpose flour

½ teaspoon baking powder

½ teaspoon salt

- Preheat oven to 350°F. Line 8″ square pan with wax paper.

- In a large bowl, cream butter and sugar until light.

- Beat in egg, orange rind and milk. Add coconut.

- Sift flour with baking powder and salt and gently add to mixture. Mix only enough to blend.

- Pour batter into prepared pan. Bake for 25 minutes.

16 SQUARES

Ginger Krinkles

⅔ cup vegetable oil

1¼ cup granulated sugar, divided

1 egg

¼ cup molasses

2 cups all purpose flour

¼ teaspoon salt

1 teaspoon ground cinnamon

1 teaspoon ground ginger

2 teaspoons baking soda

Molasses was so important to the Colonies that the founders of the state of Georgia promised each man, woman and child who would move to Georgia and "endure a year there" 64 quarts of molasses as a reward.

Until World War I molasses was the major sweetener used in the United States.

- Preheat oven to 350°F. Lightly grease cookie sheets.

- In a large bowl, mix oil and 1 cup sugar. Add egg and beat well. Stir in molasses.

- Sift together flour, salt, cinnamon, ginger and baking soda.

- Add dry ingredients to sugar mixture, stirring to blend.

- Drop dough by teaspoonfuls into ¼ cup sugar and form balls coated with sugar.

- Place balls on cookie sheet 3″ apart. Bake 8 – 10 minutes.

3 – 4 DOZEN COOKIES

Hub Chocolate Chip Cookies

Very large, thick and chewy. Absolutely the last chocolate chip recipe you'll ever need.

1 cup vegetable shortening

1 stick butter, softened

1⅓ cups granulated sugar

1 cup light brown sugar, firmly packed

4 eggs

1 tablespoon vanilla extract

1 teaspoon fresh lemon juice

2 teaspoons baking soda

1½ teaspoons salt

1 teaspoon ground cinnamon

½ cup rolled oats, regular or quick-cooking

3 cups all purpose flour

2 packages (12 ounces each) chocolate chunks or chips

2 cups chopped pecans or walnuts

- Preheat oven to 350°F. Lightly grease cookie sheets.

- In large bowl, with mixer at high speed mix shortening, butter, granulated and brown sugars until light and fluffy, about 5 minutes.

- Add eggs, one at a time, beating well after each addition.

- Beat in vanilla and lemon juice.

- In a medium bowl, stir together baking soda, salt, cinnamon, oats and flour.

- Beat flour mixture into creamed mixture until well combined.

- Stir in chocolate chunks and nuts.

- Drop ¼ cup mounds of dough onto prepared cookie sheet, 3″ apart.

- Bake 16 – 18 minutes.

3 DOZEN LARGE COOKIES

Note: Freeze well.

Cafe Congo Bars

1½ sticks unsalted butter

1 pound dark brown sugar

2 tablespoons strong instant coffee granules

1 tablespoon hot water

2 eggs

2 teaspoons vanilla extract

2 cups all purpose flour

2 teaspoons baking powder

½ teaspoon salt

1 cup semi-sweet chocolate chips

1 cup chopped walnuts

The addition of coffee gives these chewy bars a unique flavor.

- Preheat oven to 350°F. Lightly grease a 9″ × 13″ baking pan.

- Heat brown sugar and butter in large saucepan until butter melts.

- Dissolve the coffee in the hot water and stir into the butter mixture.

- Remove from heat and cool to room temperature.

- Add eggs, one at a time, beating after each addition.

- Add vanilla.

- In separate bowl, sift flour, baking powder and salt.

- Add flour mixture to butter-sugar mixture, mixing well.

- Add chocolate chips and nuts.

- Spread the batter in the prepared pan.

- Bake for 25 – 30 minutes, until lightly browned.

- Cool completely and cut into bars. Bars will harden as they cool.

24 1″ × 2″ BARS

Old Fashioned Spice Cookies

1 egg, beaten

¼ cup molasses

1¼ cups granulated sugar, divided

¾ cup vegetable oil

2 cups all purpose flour

2 teaspoons baking soda

1 teaspoon ground ginger

1 teaspoon ground cinnamon

1 teaspoon ground cloves

- Preheat oven to 350°F. Lightly grease cookie sheets.
- In a large bowl, mix together egg, molasses, 1 cup sugar and oil.
- In another large bowl, mix together flour, baking soda, ginger, cinnamon and cloves.
- Combine flour mixture with sugar mixture.
- Form cookie dough into teaspoon size balls and roll in ¼ cup granulated sugar.
- Bake for approximately 10 minutes, depending on size of balls.

50 – 60 COOKIES

Coconut Oatmeal Cookies

1 stick butter

½ cup brown sugar

½ cup granulated sugar

1 egg

¾ cup quick oatmeal

⅓ cup finely chopped pecans, or other nuts

¾ cup chopped coconut

¾ cup all purpose flour

½ teaspoon baking soda

½ teaspoon salt

½ teaspoon vanilla extract

- Preheat oven to 375°F. Lightly grease cookie sheets.
- In a large bowl, cream butter with sugars until light and fluffy. Beat in egg.
- Stir in oatmeal, nuts and coconut. Add flour, baking soda and salt. Mix in vanilla.
- Drop by rounded teaspoonfuls onto prepared cookie sheet, spacing 2″ apart, flattening cookies slightly.
- Bake for 8 minutes, until golden. Remove from cookie sheet immediately and place on wire rack to cool.

4 DOZEN COOKIES

Molasses was truly one of the most important products to early Americans. It was known as "the lifeblood of Colonial trade."
Some historians go so far as to argue that it was the Molasses Act of 1733 levied by Britain and not the tax on tea that stirred the Patriots to revolution.

For even browning when baking cookies, use a shiny cookie sheet without sides. A dark sheet absorbs the heat unevenly and can cause overbrowning, while a pan with sides deflects the heat.

Almond Raspberry Bars

¾ cup all purpose flour

3 tablespoons granulated sugar

6 tablespoons melted butter

2 tablespoons chopped almonds

1 teaspoon almond extract

⅔ cup raspberry jam

3 tablespoons butter

6 tablespoons confectioners' sugar

1 egg, beaten

½ cup chopped almonds

- Preheat oven to 350°F. Grease well and flour an 8″ × 8″ pan.

- In a large bowl, mix flour with granulated sugar.

- Blend in butter.

- Add almonds and almond extract.

- Press dough into the prepared pan.

- Spread the jam on the dough.

- In another bowl, cream together butter and confectioners' sugar.

- Add egg and mix in almonds.

- Drop this mixture by teaspoonfuls onto the jam layer, spreading gently.

- Bake for 35 minutes, or until firm to touch.

- Cool and cut into squares.

16 SQUARES

A traditional pairing of almonds and raspberries in a delicate bar cookie.

Chocolate Grand Marnier Cookies

A very special cookie that is time consuming to make. The cookies may be made in advance and frozen and the chocolate glaze may be prepared when ready to use.

COOKIES:

2½ cups all purpose flour

¼ teaspoon baking powder

¼ teaspoon salt

2 sticks unsalted butter

⅔ cup granulated sugar

1 tablespoon Grand Marnier

1 tablespoon freshly grated orange rind

1 egg

GLAZE:

1 cup semi-sweet chocolate bits

½ tablespoon vegetable shortening

½ teaspoon Grand Marnier

- Preheat oven to 350°F.

- TO PREPARE THE COOKIES: Sift together flour, baking powder and salt.

- Cream butter and sugar until light and fluffy.

- Add liqueur and orange rind.

- Add egg, then gradually add flour.

- Load cookie dough into cookie press and using flower disc, press cookies onto ungreased cookie sheets.

- Bake 10 – 12 minutes. Cool.

- TO PREPARE THE GLAZE: Melt chocolate with shortening in top of double boiler.

- When melted add liqueur, mixing well.

- Spread glaze mixture on flat side of each cookie.

- Cool.

6 DOZEN COOKIES

Tangy Lemon Cookies

1½ sticks unsalted butter

1 cup granulated sugar

1 teaspoon vanilla extract

1½ tablespoons freshly grated lemon rind (approximately 3 lemons)

¼ cup fresh lemon juice

1½ cups all purpose flour

1½ teaspoons baking powder

½ teaspoon baking soda

¼ teaspoon salt

Confectioners' sugar for sifting over cookies

A lemon will yield more juice if you place it in your microwave on high power for 15 seconds. Then roll the lemon between your palms before cutting.

- In a large bowl, cream together the butter, sugar, vanilla, lemon rind and juice, beating mixture until smooth.

- Into the bowl sift together the flour, baking powder, baking soda and salt.

- Combine butter sugar mixture with flour mixture. Blend well.

- On a piece of wax paper, form the dough into a log 1½″ in diameter, using the paper as a guide.

- Chill the log wrapped in wax paper and foil for 2 hours.

- Prepare oven to 350°F.

- Cut the log into ⅛″ slices with a sharp knife and place 2″ apart on ungreased cookie sheet.

- Bake for 8 – 10 minutes or until the edges are just golden.

- Transfer the cookies with a metal spatula to racks to cool.

- Sift confectioners' sugar over cookies lightly.

50 COOKIES

Note: *The dough may be made up to 3 months in advance and kept frozen, well wrapped.*

South Pacific Snowballs

An interesting variation on the classic snowball cookie.

1 tablespoon vegetable shortening

1 stick unsalted butter, softened

1 cup all purpose flour

4 tablespoons Frangelico or light rum

1 teaspoon vanilla extract

¼ teaspoon salt

1¼ cups finely chopped macadamia nuts

1 cup confectioners' sugar

- Lightly grease cookie sheets with vegetable shortening.
- In a large bowl, with mixer cream butter.
- Continue beating and gradually add the flour, Frangelico, vanilla and salt. Blend well.
- Add nuts and beat at low speed until blended well.
- Wrap dough in plastic wrap and refrigerate for 1 hour.
- Preheat oven to 300°F.
- Form dough into ¾″ diameter balls by hand.
- Place balls on cookie sheet 2″ apart.
- Bake on middle rack of oven for 35 minutes.
- Remove from oven. Cool slightly and roll in confectioners' sugar.
- When completely cool, roll in sugar again.

3 DOZEN COOKIES

Copp's Hill Burial Ground

Another of the Puritans' famous burial grounds is Copp's Hill Burial Ground located in the North End. Once the site of a windmill, the cemetery was established in 1659-60, taking its name from William Copp, the owner of the land. The site, which was originally on much higher ground than today, provided a strategic vantage point from which British troops could overlook all of Boston Harbor and the entrance to the Charles River. From here, facing Bunker Hill across the water in 1775, the British organized their artillery and fired upon Charlestown.

In Copp's Hill Burial Ground the slate headstones of the famous ministers, Cotton, Samuel and Increase Mather can be found. Cotton Mather, the fiery pastor and persecutor of witches, once said of Boston, ''Almost a Hell upon earth, a city full of lies and murders and blasphemies; a dismal picture and emblem of Hell.'' Here too lies the builder of the U.S.S. Constitution, Edmund Hall, as well as Robert Newman, sexton of the Old North Church. He helped to hang the famous lanterns for Paul Revere, ''One if by land, two if by sea.''

Arlington Iced Tea

The English firm of Messrs. Davison, Newman and Coryson whose tea was thrown overboard on the chilly December night in 1773, is still in business producing fine teas.

½ cup boiling water

1¼ cups granulated sugar

Juice of 3 lemons

3 mint sprigs

2½ quarts boiling water

2 heaping tablespoons loose tea

GARNISH:

Mint sprigs

- Pour ½ cup boiling water over sugar, lemon juice and mint, stirring well until sugar dissolves.

- Pour 2½ quarts boiling water over tea.

- Let both mixtures stand for 20 minutes.

- Strain the sugar mixture into the tea, then strain the combined mixture again, making sure all the sugar is included.

- Cool and serve chilled with lots of ice cubes and mint sprig garnish.

Berkeley Lemon Mint Drink

A refreshing summer drink that's so easy to have on hand.

2 cups granulated sugar

2½ cups water

Juice of 6 lemons

Juice of 4 oranges

Grated rind of 1 orange

1½ cups fresh mint leaves, chopped

Cold water

- Boil together sugar and water for 15 minutes.

- Stir in the lemon and orange juices and orange rind.

- Pour over mint in 2 quart bowl. Let steep at room temperature 1 hour.

- Strain before serving.

- To serve add ⅓ cup lemon-mint syrup to 1 cup of cold water.

8 – 10 CUPS

Note: May be stored for one month in the refrigerator.

Clarendon Happy Times Punch

2 cans (6 ounces each) frozen lemonade concentrate

1 can (6 ounces) frozen orange juice concentrate

9 cups cold water

5 pints pineapple sherbert

1 quart vanilla ice cream

GARNISH:

Orange, lemon and/or lime slices

- Combine frozen concentrates and water.

- Place sherbet and ice cream in bottom of punch bowl. Break into small chunks.

- Add juices and water to punch bowl.

- Stir punch until sherbet and ice cream are partially melted.

- Garnish with orange, lemon and lime slices.

5 QUARTS

Note: Pineapple sorbet may be substituted for the sherbert.

A rich, frappe-like drink that's popular with both children and adults.

Did you know that Ben Franklin was born at 17 Milk St. in Boston? Today, you will find a bust of Ben Franklin on the 2nd floor outside of the building, marking this location.

Dartmouth Fish House Punch

2 cups brandy

1 cup light rum

1 cup dark rum

½ cup peach brandy

1 cup fresh lemon juice

3 tablespoons confectioners' sugar

1 quart club soda, chilled

- In a large punch bowl, combine brandy, light and dark rums, peach brandy, lemon juice, sugar and soda.

- Chill, using a decorative ice mold or ice cubes.

8 – 10 SERVINGS OR 20 4-OUNCE CUPS

A perfect punch for an open house or cocktail party at holiday time.

Exeter Spiced Wine

A warming drink to be served by the fireside after a day of skiing.

1 gallon burgundy wine

2 quarts water

2 lemons, sliced

2½ cups granulated sugar

18 whole cloves

8 cinnamon sticks

1 orange, sliced and squeezed

- In a large pot, combine wine, water, lemons, sugar, cloves, cinnamon sticks and orange.

- Simmer on low at least 20 minutes.

- Remove cloves and cinnamon sticks before serving.

- Pour into warmed mugs.

1½ GALLONS

Fairfield Buttered and Steeped Rum

Rum was another product enjoyed by the Colonists that was made principally from molasses.

It was estimated that in pre-revolutionary days, men, women and children consumed an average of four gallons of rum a year.

2 sticks butter, softened (do not use margarine)

1 cup dark brown sugar, firmly packed

¼ cup honey

2 teaspoons ground cinnamon

1 teaspoon freshly grated nutmeg

½ teaspoon ground cloves

4 cups light rum

GARNISH:

6 cinnamon sticks

- In processor or with mixer, cream butter and sugar until fluffy.

- Add honey, cinnamon, nutmeg and cloves and beat well.

- Heat rum to steaming. Do not boil.

- Divide butter-sugar mixture between 6 mugs.

- Pour steaming rum over mixture and stir gently with cinnamon sticks.

6 SERVINGS

Gloucester Cinnamon Cider

1 quart apple cider

4 ounces bourbon

4 cinnamon sticks

- In a medium saucepan, bring cider and cinnamon sticks to a simmer, cook 2 minutes.

- Pour into warmed mugs and stir in bourbon.

4 SERVINGS

Hereford Egg Nog

6 egg yolks

¼ cup granulated sugar

3 tablespoons rum extract

1 teaspoon vanilla extract

1½ cups chilled cream

6 egg whites

5 tablespoons granulated sugar

GARNISH:

Freshly grated nutmeg

- With mixer beat together egg yolks, ¼ cup sugar, rum and vanilla extracts until thick and lemon-colored.

- Add cream gradually and continue to beat until blended. Set aside.

- Beat egg whites until frothy.

- Add 5 tablespoons sugar, gradually beating until stiff peaks form.

- Fold whites into yolk mixture until blended.

- Chill.

- Pour in punch bowl and gently mix before serving. Sprinkle freshly grated nutmeg on top.

16 SERVINGS

As you explore Boston and its harbor area, you're apt to come across a giant wooden milk bottle. This "2,000 gallon-capacity landmark" stands next to the Children's Museum at Museum Wharf.

It was moved here from Taunton, Massachusetts years ago. It's a favorite gathering spot and foodstand in the summertime.

And speaking of milk, each year the Massachusetts Dietetic Association (MDA) sponsors the Boston Milk Run.

This annual 10K race about town is always held the weekend before the Boston Marathon.

The Milk Run is another well-known rite of spring in Boston.

The race draws thousands of runners from all over the country and, even if you're not a health fanatic, this is a great event to support because all of the proceeds go to charity.

Massachusetts Avenue Banana Smoothie

1 banana, sliced

½ cup plain yogurt

½ cup orange juice

3 tablespoons honey

GARNISH:

Freshly Grated Nutmeg

- In a food processor or blender combine the banana, yogurt, orange juice and honey and process until smooth.
- Pour into a glass and garnish with nutmeg.

SERVES 1

Charlesgate Hot Chocolate

4 cups milk

3 ounces unsweetened chocolate

¾ cup granulated sugar

½ teaspoon ground cinnamon

¾ cup dark rum

GARNISH:

¼ teaspoon cinnamon and 1 tablespoon granulated sugar combined.

- In a small saucepan combine milk, chocolate, sugar and cinnamon. Cook over medium heat stirring constantly for 5 minutes or until chocolate is melted and sugar is dissolved.
- Add rum and heat mixture for 1 minute.
- In a food processor or blender process mixture until foamy.
- Divide mixture among 4 mugs.
- Garnish with cinnamon sugar mixture.

4 SERVINGS

Charlestown Navy Yard/U.S.S. Constitution

Round about the Freedom Trail, over the bridge and into Charlestown is the Charlestown Navy Yard and the U.S.S. Constitution. Once one of the most active navy yards on the East Coast, Charlestown Navy Yard was closed by President Richard M. Nixon in 1974.

Today, however, the activity surrounds our country's oldest commissioned U.S. Navy ship. The Constitution is the oldest commissioned warship afloat in the world. During the summer months long lines of tourists wait to visit "Old Ironsides." The nickname dates from the War of 1812 and a battle with the British frigate HMS Guerriere. So little damage was done by cannonballs fired at the hull that one sailor proclaimed, "Huzza! Her sides are made of iron!" Finished and launched in 1797 at a cost of $302,718, the U.S.S. Constitution, a 44-gun frigate, fought in forty battles and never saw defeat.

The ship has been restored and maintained over the years, thanks to the initial petition of Oliver Wendell Holmes in 1830. Anyone may go aboard and view firsthand the crew's quarters, captain's cabin, the cannon, the sick bay and rum barrels — just as they were when the ship traveled the high seas. Every year, the Constitution is turned about in the harbor, and the ship's guns salute the nation on the Fourth of July.

CRANBERRIES

The Cranberry

The cranberry is one of North America's three native fruits (the others are blueberries and Concord grapes), and even today are grown almost exclusively in the United States. Originally spelled "craneberry," the fruit takes its name from the pink blossoms which are produced in July and resemble the head of a crane. The middle "e" was dropped probably in the 1800's.

The native Americans used the tart fruit for medicine and dyes, and mixed it with venison to make pemmican, a dried food that could be stored for use in winter. The Pilgrims found the fruit an excellent remedy against scurvy.

Cranberry cultivation began on Cape Cod in 1812, and the man most responsible for modern cranberry cultivation was Henry Hall from Dennis, Massachusetts.

Cranberries are grown on low-lying vines planted in peat bogs. A thin layer of sand on top of the bogs acts like a mulch, burying dead matter and promoting new growth. Vines may take between three to five years to mature before producing a marketable crop. Once the vines bear fruit, however, bogs can produce far more than one hundred years if they are properly maintained.

The cranberry bogs are flooded in the winter to protect the tender vines from freezing and again in the fall to float the berries for picking. Drainage ditches carry off the excess water. In the summer, pink blossoms appear on the vines and millions of honey bees are turned loose to pollinate the flowers.

Harvesting of the ripened berries begins after Labor Day and ends in late November. Like maple syrup, high-quality cranberries need cold nights and warm sunny days to ripen. Cranberries are harvested by one of two distinct techniques. In dry harvesting, used for cranberries destined for noncommercial users, a mechanical picker combs the fruit from the vine. The berries are collected in burlap sacks, loaded into bins, and then taken to a plant. Only dry-picked cranberries can be sold as fresh fruit in states that grow cranberries.

Almost 80 percent of the cranberries are harvested by the wet method. In wet harvesting, bogs are flooded to a depth of approximately two feet. Machines known as water reels, or "egg beaters," are driven over the bogs, churning the water and shaking the ripe berries loose. The cranberries float to the surface and are drawn together; they are then lifted into trucks for delivery to a receiving station. Cranberries wet-picked are used for processed foods.

The processing of cranberries relies on a machine designed over one hundred years ago. The fresh berries, taken directly from the bogs, are loaded into the top of a wooden belt-driven machine called a "bouncer." The berries drop through a series of wooden barriers. The principle is that good berries will drop, and they do. Engineers have tried to invent a more modern device to test for freshness but nothing has been found to work as well as this old machine.

Massachusetts produces more than 50 percent of the nation's cranberry crop. The harvest in 1988 set a record, with a total of 1.825 million barrels of cranberries. There are approximately 11,800 acres of cranberry bogs in Massachusetts, and cranberries recently passed dairy goods as the leading agricultural product in Massachusetts.

Most people associate the cranberry with holiday dinners, and the holiday seasons are certainly the most popular time of the year for cranberries. The Thanksgiving condiment, canned cranberry, is over 75 years old. But the cranberry is a very versatile fruit and mixes well with almost everything. Here are several recipes to expand your list of cranberry dishes.

Sugar-Glazed Scallop Ka-bobs with Cranberry Dipping Sauce

*OCEAN SPRAY
CRANBERRIES, INC.
225 Water Street
Plymouth,
Massachusetts 02360*

KA-BOBS:

2 red bell peppers cut into ½″ pieces

1 pound scallops

1 onion cut into ½″ pieces

1 green pepper cut into ½″ pieces

4 tablespoons butter

¼ cup light brown sugar

2 tablespoons fresh lime juice

SAUCE:

1 can (8 ounces) jellied cranberry sauce

2 tablespoons apple cider vinegar

2 tablespoons soy sauce

1 garlic clove, finely minced

1 teaspoon Dijon mustard

¼ teaspoon ground ginger

⅛ teaspoon Cayenne pepper

GARNISH:

Chopped scallions

- Preheat broiler or grill.

- Thread 6″ skewers in the following order: red pepper, scallop, onion, scallop, green pepper, scallop, red pepper.

- In a saucepan, combine butter, brown sugar and lime juice and heat over medium heat until butter is melted and ingredients are thoroughly blended.

- Brush the ka-bobs with the sugar mixture.

- If using broiler, arrange ka-bobs in a broiler pan. Broil or grill 2 – 3 minutes, turn and continue cooking for 2 – 3 more minutes. Scallops should be opaque and lightly browned.

- TO PREPARE THE SAUCE: In a small saucepan, mix cranberry sauce, vinegar, soy sauce, garlic, mustard, ginger and pepper.

- Boil, reduce heat, cover and let simmer for 5 minutes.

- To serve, arrange skewers on a tray with the warm cranberry dipping sauce in a separate bowl.

- Garnish ka-bobs with chopped scallions.

10 – 12 SKEWERS

Cranberry Banana Bread

¼ cup butter

1 cup granulated sugar

1 egg

2 cups all purpose flour

3 teaspoons baking powder

½ teaspoon ground cinnamon

½ teaspoon salt

1 cup mashed banana

½ cup milk

1 teaspoon grated orange rind

1 cup fresh cranberries, coarsely chopped

½ cup chopped walnuts

- Preheat oven to 350°F. Grease a 9″ × 5″ × 3″ loaf pan.
- In a large bowl, cream butter and sugar, add the egg and beat well.
- Sift together the flour, baking powder, cinnamon and salt.
- In a small bowl, combine the bananas, milk and orange rind.
- Add the dry ingredients and banana mixture alternately to the creamed mixture.
- Fold in cranberries and walnuts.
- Pour into prepared loaf pan.
- Bake for 1 hour or until cake tester inserted in center comes out clean.

Note: Freezes well.

A traditional Autumn bread both savory and sweet. Makes a perfect holiday gift.

Orange-Cranberry Bread

2 cups all purpose flour, sifted

1 cup granulated sugar

½ teaspoon salt

1½ teaspoons baking powder

½ teaspoon baking soda

1 cup coarsely chopped pecans or walnuts

1 cup fresh whole cranberries

2 tablespoons vegetable oil

Hot water

2 tablespoons grated orange rind

½ cup freshly squeezed orange juice

1 egg, slightly beaten

- Preheat oven to 325°F. Grease 9″ × 5″ × 3″ loaf pan.
- In a large bowl, sift together flour, sugar, salt, baking powder and baking soda.
- In a small bowl, combine nuts and cranberries. Toss with ½ cup of flour mixture.
- Pour oil in measuring cup and add enough hot water to make ¾ cup.
- Combine orange rind and juice with oil-water mixture.
- Stir egg into flour mixture, just enough to moisten.
- Gently stir orange mixture, cranberries and nuts into flour mixture.
- Pour batter into prepared pan.
- Bake for 1 hour.
- Cool completely before removing from pan.
- Wrap in foil and store in refrigerator, or freeze.

1 LOAF

Braised Beef with Cranberries

2 teaspoons freshly ground black pepper

2 pounds stewing beef, cut into 1" cubes

3 tablespoons olive oil

2 large garlic cloves, minced

2 medium onions, chopped

1 cup thinly sliced carrots

2 tablespoons red wine vinegar

2 tablespoons tomato paste

¾ cup dry red wine

¾ cup beef stock

½ cup light brown sugar

2 cups fresh cranberries, reserving a few whole berries for garnish

2 tablespoons all purpose flour

GARNISH:

Cranberries

- Sprinkle pepper over beef.

- In a large saucepan or Dutch oven, heat oil.

- Brown beef on all sides.

- Add garlic, onions and carrots.

- In a medium bowl, mix together vinegar, tomato paste, wine, beef stock and brown sugar.

- Pour mixture over beef and vegetables.

- Bring to a boil, then reduce to a simmer, cover and cook until meat is tender, about 2 hours.

- Chop cranberries coarsely and combine with flour.

- Add berries to pan, stir well and cook for 10 minutes uncovered.

- Garnish with whole cranberries.

5 – 6 SERVINGS

An unusual combination- hearty and tart.

Herbed Mustard Chicken Breasts

*OCEAN SPRAY
CRANBERRIES, INC.
225 Water Street
Plymouth,
Massachusetts 02360*

2 whole chicken breasts, halved

Salt and freshly ground black pepper, to taste

2 tablespoons vegetable oil

1 cup firmly packed fresh herbs: chervil, parsley, dill, chives and basil, cleaned and stemmed

2½ cups lightly packed fresh bread or brioche crumbs

2 tablespoons Pommery mustard

2 tablespoons butter, melted

1 shallot, chopped

¾ cup strong chicken stock

1 cup dry white wine

¾ cup heavy cream

1⅛ cups beef stock

1 tablespoon honey

¾ cup cranberries, fresh frozen or fresh

1 cup granulated sugar

GARNISH:

12 chervil leaves

- Preheat oven to 350°F.

- TO PREPARE THE CHICKEN: Sprinkle breasts lightly with salt and pepper.

- In large skillet, heat oil.

- Add chicken breasts to skillet 2 at a time and cook until lightly browned on both sides.

- Remove chicken from skillet and set aside.

- Repeat with remaining chicken.

- Place chicken in shallow pan. Bake for 5 minutes. Increase heat to broil.

- TO PREPARE THE HERBED MUSTARD COATING: Pulse mixed herbs in food processor until coarsely chopped.

Continued on next page

- Add bread crumbs, mustard and butter to herbs. Pulse until ingredients are combined and herbs are finely chopped. (If food processor is not available, finely chop herbs and combine with bread crumbs, mustard and butter.)

- Pat herbed mustard mixture onto top side of chicken.

- Place in preheated broiler until lightly browned.

- TO PREPARE THE SHALLOT CREAM SAUCE: In a medium saucepan, combine shallot, chicken stock and all except 2 tablespoons wine. Simmer to reduce volume to 2 tablespoons.

- Add cream and simmer until mixture thickens. Season to taste with salt and pepper.

- TO PREPARE THE BROWN SAUCE: In small saucepan, heat beef stock and honey. Simmer until thickened, stirring occasionally.

- Caramelize cranberries by heating in skillet with sugar and remaining 2 tablespoons wine.

- Stir frequently and watch carefully to prevent burning.

- To serve, pour some of shallot cream sauce in center of each of 4 serving plates. Top with chicken breast and spoon on brown sauce.

- Garnish with glazed cranberries and chervil leaves..

4 SERVINGS

Did you know that Charlestown is older than Boston? It was founded in 1629 by a handful of settlers sent by the Massachusetts Bay Company to inhabit the company's holdings in New England.

The group consisted of just ten men, their families and their servants. They were joined one year later by John Winthrop, the first Governor of the colony, and his shipload of Puritans.

Their first years were made difficult by epidemics, fear of Indians, and a water supply so foul that it drove Winthrop to move his colony across the Charles River to a purer spring.

Thus, it was Charlestown's bad water that "caused" the founding of Boston.

Excerpted from The Official Bicentennial Guidebook, *1976, p. 143.*

Warm Spiced Cranberry Punch

½ cup granulated sugar

1 cup water

½ teaspoon whole cloves

4 cinnamon sticks

2 cups cranberry juice

½ cup fresh lemon juice

1 cup freshly squeezed orange juice

1 quart ginger ale

GARNISH:

Slices of lemon and orange

- In a large pan, combine sugar, water, cloves and cinnamon sticks. Bring to a boil and cook for 5 minutes.
- Strain and let cool.
- Combine cooled sugar mixture with cranberry, lemon and orange juices. Heat again.
- Before mixture boils add ginger ale. Let it boil and add lemon and orange slices.
- Serve warm.

12 SERVINGS

Cranberry Strawberry Mold

1 cup boiling cranberry juice

1 package (3 ounces) strawberry jello

1 cup chopped cranberries

1 pint ripe fresh strawberries, crushed and lightly sugared or 1 package (10 ounces) frozen strawberries, partially defrosted

1 Granny Smith apple peeled, cored and chopped

1 teaspoon grated orange rind

- Grease a 6 cup ring mold.
- In a medium saucepan, heat cranberry juice to boiling. Put jello in large bowl and pour hot cranberry juice on jello. Stir to dissolve.
- Stir in cranberries and strawberries. Add apple and grated orange rind.
- Pour into prepared ring mold. Chill 3 – 4 hours until firm or overnight. Unmold on large platter.

6 – 8 SERVINGS

Note: Serve with mayonnaise mixed with a little sour cream.

Cranberry Bread Pudding

1 loaf French bread, day old, approximately 6 cups of chunky
   pieces

1 cup cranberries, coarsely chopped

1 cup nuts, coarsely chopped (hazel, walnut, pecan, etc.)

2 cups milk

2 cups cream (any style)

3 eggs

1 cup light brown sugar

½ cup granulated sugar

1 tablespoon vanilla extract

¼ cup dark Barbados rum, or to taste

Maple syrup or hard sauce

- Grease a 9″ × 13″ × 2″ pan.

- In a large mixing bowl, combine bread pieces with cranberries and nuts, pouring milk and cream over all to soak for 1
  hour.

- Preheat oven to 325°F.

- In separate bowl, beat the eggs.

- Add both sugars, vanilla and rum, stirring into the bread
  mixture.

- Pour into prepared pan and bake on middle oven rack, uncovered, for 1 hour or until browned and set.

- Let cool slightly before serving, slice into squares and top
  with maple syrup or hard sauce.

8 – 10 SERVINGS

When buying fresh cranberries it is useful to know that a 12-ounce bag contains 3¼ cups. Cranberries should be picked over to remove any stems or leaves.

Cranberries freeze well. Keep some in the freezer to make your favorite cranberry recipes in the summer.

Cranberry Chutney

A traditional accompaniment for poultry or ham. Spicy and interesting.

1 cup chopped onion

1 cup apple cider

1 cup dark brown sugar

¾ cup granulated sugar

¾ cup apple cider vinegar

2 tart apples, diced

1 teaspoon ground ginger

1 teaspoon allspice

½ teaspoon mace

1 teaspoon ground cinnamon

Rind of 2 oranges, grated

1½ cups cranberries

½ cup raisins

Juice of 2 oranges, strained

1 cup chopped walnuts (optional)

- In a large saucepan, simmer onions with apple cider and sugars for 30 minutes.
- Stir in vinegar, apples, ginger, allspice, mace, cinnamon and orange rind. Simmer for 30 minutes more.
- Add cranberries, raisins and orange juice.
- Boil slowly for 10 minutes or until cranberries burst. Stir occasionally.
- Add nuts, if desired. Pour into sterile jars and store in freezer.

10 – 12 CUPS

Cranberry Sorbet

FROSTED CRANBERRIES:

In a pie plate with a fork, beat 1 egg white slightly. Onto wax paper, measure ¼ cup extra fine granulated sugar. Coat 1 cup cranberries with egg white, then coat cranberries completely with sugar.

Place frosted cranberries on wire rack over wax paper to dry, at least one hour.

1½ quarts fresh cranberries

7 cups water, divided

Juice of 3 oranges

Juice of 1½ lemons

1½ cups granulated sugar

- In a large saucepan, boil cranberries in 4 cups of water until soft. Cool and strain, discarding pulp.
- Add juice of oranges and lemons to purée.
- In a separate saucepan, boil sugar with 3 cups water. Reduce heat and simmer for 5 minutes.
- Mix syrup and purée.
- Use ice cream maker if available*, if not, freeze mixture in ice cube trays until barely frozen.
- Place mixture in large bowl and beat with hand mixer.
- Refreeze in trays and beat again with mixer when barely frozen. Freeze.
- Just before serving remove from freezer for a few minutes.

* For ice cream maker, follow manufacturer's directions.

2 QUARTS

Bunker Hill Monument

People can see it from all over Boston: the Bunker Hill Monument in Charlestown towers 221 feet. Visitors can climb the 294 steps to the top for a splendid view of Boston Harbor and the surrounding areas.

The site and obelisk commemorate the unyielding spirit of Yankee soldiers in their fight against the British on June 17, 1775. In what is known as the Battle of Bunker Hill, though actually fought on Breed's Hill, 1,500 colonial minutemen, fought valiantly against the British Regular Army although outnumbered 3 to 1. They held fire so as not to waste precious gunpowder, following Colonial William Prescott's command, "Don't fire until you see the whites of their eyes!" By the end of the day, the British had suffered more than 1,000 casualties. The colonials were forced to retreat, but this battle did much to shore up the spirit of our fighting men. It was a great moral victory for the colonial militia.

The Statue of Colonel William Prescott

On the south side of the Bunker Hill Monument is the bronze statue of a man with a sword. Carved in Rome and cast in the United States by the American sculptor, William Story, the 7 foot statue honors Colonel William Prescott.

Hot Maine Crab Custard with Chive and Tomato

*The Bostonian Hotel
Faneuil Hall
Marketplace
Boston, MA. 02109*

CUSTARD:

4 eggs

2 cups heavy cream

**Salt and freshly ground
black pepper, to taste**

7 ounces Maine crabmeat

**5 tablespoons chopped
chives**

SAUCE:

¼ cup heavy cream

1 stick unsalted butter

**Salt and freshly ground
black pepper, to taste**

Juice of 1 lemon

GARNISH:

**3 tablespoons diced tomato,
peeled and seeded**

**2 tablespoons chopped
chives**

- Preheat oven to 325°F. Butter 4 ramekins well.

- TO PREPARE THE CUSTARD: Whisk eggs and cream together until thoroughly mixed.

- Season mixture with salt and pepper.

- Add crabmeat and chives to mixture.

- Pour egg mixture into prepared ramekins. Place ramekins in a water bath and bake for 20 minutes or until custard sets.

- TO PREPARE THE SAUCE: In a small heavy saucepan, reduce cream by half.

- Gradually whisk butter into cream.

- Season with salt, pepper and lemon juice.

- When the custards are set, run a knife around the rim of each ramekin.

- Gently unmold custards onto a warm plate.

- Sauce lightly, and garnish with tomato and chives.

4 SERVINGS

Grilled Lobsters with Mango Salsa

1½ pound lobster

SALSA:

2 tablespoons olive oil

1 tablespoon fresh lime juice

1 garlic clove, minced

¼ teaspoon salt

1 large ripe mango, peeled, cut into ¼" cubes

2 tablespoons minced sweet red onion

2 tablespoons minced white onion

1 green onion, minced

1 tablespoon chopped fresh basil, including stems

1 teaspoon chopped fresh mint

1 teaspoon minced hot chili

- Steam lobster in 2" boiling water in large pot for 17 minutes.

- Remove from pot. Drain and split body and tail with a large sharp knife.

- Crack claws with knife for ease in removing meat.

- Preheat grill.

- Finish cooking, approximately 6 minutes, on grill.

- TO MAKE THE SALSA: Whisk together oil, lime juice, garlic and salt.

- To the oil mixture, add mango, onions, basil, mint and chili to create a relish texture.

- When lobster is finished cooking, fill cavity with mango salsa.

- Serve immediately.

1 SERVING

Boston Lobster House
256 Commerical Street
Boston, MA. 02109

White Gazpacho

The Boston Park Plaza
Hotel and Towers
50 Park Plaza
Boston, MA. 02117

7 green tomatoes, cored

1 small onion

2 garlic cloves

1 cucumber, peeled and seeded

1 yellow pepper

¼ cup olive oil

¼ cup white vinegar

½ teaspoon cumin

Pinch cayenne pepper or hot pepper sauce

Salt and freshly ground black pepper, to taste

½ cup heavy cream

GARNISH:

Slices of cucumber and sour cream

OR

Diced cucumbers, green and yellow peppers and minced fresh chives

- In a food processor, place the tomatoes, onion, garlic, cucumber and yellow pepper.

- Purée. Transfer vegetables to a blender and purée again in small batches, until smooth.

- Add oil, vinegar, cumin, cayenne, salt and pepper. Let stand in refrigerator overnight.

- Add heavy cream.

- Garnish with cucumber slices and a teaspoonful of sour cream, or diced cucumbers, green and yellow peppers and chives.

4 – 6 SERVINGS

Sautéed Fillet of Sole with Marinated Peppers and Cherrystones

14 ounces fresh cherrystone clams

1 cup white wine

3 tablespoons celery, diced

1½ tablespoons green pepper, diced

1½ tablespoons red pepper, diced

1½ tablespoons yellow pepper, diced

3 teaspoons olive oil

3 teaspoons fish stock

½ teaspoon tarragon or balsamic vinegar

Salt and freshly ground black pepper, to taste

4 fresh fillets of sole, approximately 6 ounces each, skinned and de-boned

Milk for dredging

Flour for dredging

2½ tablespoons butter

2 teaspoons vegetable oil

The Boston Park Plaza Hotel and Towers
50 Park Plaza
Boston, MA. 02117

- Preheat oven to 275°F.

- In a sauce pan, place cherrystone clams in ¼″ boiling water and wine. Steam until shells open, approximately 8 – 10 minutes.

- Remove clams from shells and set aside.

- Mix diced celery, green, red and yellow peppers with oil, fish stock and vinegar.

- Add the cherrystones and salt and pepper. Set aside.

- Sprinkle fillets with salt and pepper and, if desired, dip in milk and flour to dredge.

- Heat butter and oil in a large sauté pan.

- Place fillets in pan and sauté quickly on both sides until golden brown.

- Place pan in oven for 10 minutes.

- Arrange each fillet on a warmed dinner plate and garnish with the marinated cherrystones and peppers.

4 SERVINGS

Corn Oysters

The Colony
384 Boylston Street
Boston, MA. 02116

6 ears fresh corn

1 egg, separated

1 extra egg yolk

¼ cup flour

Salt and freshly ground pepper, to taste

Pinch of cayenne pepper

Pinch of cream of tartar

Vegetable oil, for shallow frying

- Shuck the corn.
- Take 2 ears, and using a small knife, split each row down the center of the kernels.
- Scrape out pulp and milky liquid and put in a bowl.
- Using the knife, cut the kernels off of remaining 4 ears. Add them to pulp and milky liquid in bowl.
- Stir in the 2 egg yolks. Then add flour and a generous pinch of salt, pepper and cayenne.
- In another bowl, beat the egg white with the cream of tartar and a pinch of salt until the egg white holds stiff peaks.
- Fold egg white into corn mixture, taking care not to overmix.
- In a deep skillet, heat 1" of oil. When oil is very hot, add heaping tablespoons of the batter to the oil.
- Fry fritters until golden brown on undersides. Turn over and brown other sides.
- Drain corn oysters on paper towels. Sprinkle lightly with salt and serve with spicy tartar sauce.

Continued on next page

SPICY TARTAR SAUCE:

½ cup homemade mayonnaise

2 tablespoons piccalilli

1 tablespoon chopped capers

1 tablespoon chopped fresh herbs (chives, tarragon, parsley)

1 tablespoon cider vinegar

1 tablespoon lemon juice

1 jalapeño pepper, seeded and chopped

Generous pinch of cayenne pepper

Salt and freshly ground black pepper, to taste

- In a bowl, whisk together the mayonnaise, piccalilli, capers and herbs.
- Gradually whisk in the vinegar and lemon juice until mixture is smooth.
- Add chopped pepper, cayenne and salt.
- Add more vinegar to make a dressing that is the consistency of a dipping sauce, taste for seasoning.
- Spoon the tartar sauce into a bowl and serve at once.

12 – 16 SERVINGS

The Colony
384 Boylston Street
Boston, MA. 02116

Dini's Famous Broiled Fresh Scrod

Dini's Sea Grill
94 Tremont Street
Boston, MA. 02155

4 fillets young cod, approximately 12 ounces each

¾ cup corn oil

1 cup seasoned bread crumbs

GARNISH:

4 lemon wedges

Minced fresh parsley

1 cup drawn butter*

- Preheat broiler.
- Dip the fillets in oil and coat with the seasoned bread crumbs.
- Place fish in pan and broil until golden brown.
- Remove from the broiler.
- Reduce heat to bake at 350°F. and return fish to oven until done, approximately 5 minutes.
- Serve garnished with lemon wedges, parsley and drawn butter.

4 SERVINGS

* Drawn butter is made by melting 1 cup butter, letting it cool, and skimming off the butter fat from the top.

Chicken Breast with Goat Cheese and Basil

4 (6 ounce) chicken breasts, split, skinned and boned

Salt and freshly ground black pepper, to taste

5 ounces fresh goat cheese

12 leaves fresh basil, finely chopped

1 pound caul fat*

6 ounces Madeira

1 tablespoon minced shallots

16 ounces chicken glacé (very reduced chicken stock)

1 stick unsalted butter

Four Seasons Hotel
200 Boylston Street
Boston, MA. 02116

- Season chicken breasts with salt and pepper.

- Preheat sauté pan over medium-high heat and then quickly sear chicken to golden brown all over. Cool to room temperature.

- Preheat oven to 400°F.

- Using a sharp knife, cut a pocket in each breast.

- Crumble goat cheese and mix with basil.

- Stuff each pocket with approximately 1 tablespoon of the mixture.

- Soak the caul fat in cold water and allow to open up.

- Cut into 6″ × 6″ squares and lay flat.

- Place a chicken breast in the center of each square and fold caul fat over twice to completely enclose the breast. Repeat with other breasts.

- Place breasts in a heat-proof dish.

- In a medium size saucepan, reduce Madeira and shallots by half.

- Add chicken glacé and reduce again by half. Remove from heat and keep warm.

- Place chicken in oven and bake for approximately 15 minutes.

- TO FINISH SAUCE: Whisk in butter and adjust seasonings.

- Serve chicken breast on top of sauce with baby vegetables.

4 SERVINGS

* Available from a butcher

Scallops Ethan

Hampshire House
84 Beacon Street
Boston, MA. 02108

3 cups broccoli purée

2 pounds sea scallops, sliced

6 ounces clarified butter

3 ounces freshly squeezed lemon juice

4 ounces brandy

Pinch salt

Pinch white pepper

Flour for dredging

- Lightly dredge half the scallops in flour. Quickly sauté in a very hot pan with half the butter.

- Remove from pan and repeat with remaining scallops and butter.

- Return all scallops to pan. Add brandy and flambé.

- Add salt, pepper and lemon juice.

- Spoon over broccoli purée.

BROCCOLI PURÉE

3 cups cooked broccoli

¼ cup heavy cream

4 tablespoons softened butter

¼ cup grated Parmesan cheese

Salt, freshly ground black pepper and nutmeg, to taste

- Combine all ingredients in a food processor, fitted with the steel blade.

6 SERVINGS

Note: If you must reheat this purée, do so very carefully over hot water.

Grilled Stuffed Shrimp

1 pound jumbo shrimp (12 per pound)

6 thin slices Provolone cheese

6 ounces herb cheese

1 bunch scallions, green part only, sliced

Salt and freshly ground black pepper, to taste

12 slices bacon

- Preheat grill.
- Peel and clean shrimp. Cut from head end three-quarters of the way to tail.
- Lay Provolone cheese flat and cut in half.
- On each half piece of cheese spread 1 tablespoon of herb cheese.
- Sprinkle green part of scallions on top of herb cheese.
- Add salt and pepper. Fold cheese in half so that all the Provolone is on the outside.
- Place cheese inside the cut shrimp.
- Wrap slice of bacon completely around shrimp, making sure all of shrimp is covered.
- Grill each side approximately 3 minutes.

4 SERVINGS OF 3 SHRIMP EACH

Harvard Club of Boston
374 Commonwealth
Avenue
Boston, MA. 02215

Pan Blackened Scallops with Pesto Sauce

Harvard Club of Boston
374 Commonwealth
Avenue
Boston, MA. 02215

BLACKENING MIXTURE:

½ cup olive oil

2 teaspoons paprika

2 teaspoons garlic powder

1 teaspoon cayenne pepper

1 teaspoon white pepper

2 tablespoons honey

1½ pounds extra large sea
scallops

SAUCE:

1 bunch fresh basil, stems
removed

1 tablespoon garlic, minced

¼ cup pine nuts

¼ cup freshly grated
Parmesan cheese

2 tablespoons olive oil

Salt and freshly ground
black pepper, to taste

¼ cup heavy cream

- TO PREPARE BLACK FISH SEASONING: Mix together olive oil, paprika, garlic powder, cayenne, white pepper and honey.

- Coat scallops with blackening mixture.

- In hot cast iron pan, cook each side of scallop for 1 minute.

- In blender, combine basil leaves, garlic, pine nuts, Parmesan, olive oil and salt and pepper and blend until smooth.

- In saucepan, heat sauce with cream.

- Serve scallops on Pesto Sauce.

4 SERVINGS

Roast Rack of Lamb with Tarragon Glaze

MARINADE:

1 quart olive oil

½ head of garlic, peeled and minced

4 mint leaves

3 bay leaves

2 lemons, sliced

1 hotel rack of lamb, French trim, cut in 4 portions

SAUCE:

2 pounds lamb trimmings and bones

4 celery stalks, coarsely chopped

4 onions, coarsely chopped

4 carrots, coarsely chopped

2 heads of garlic, peeled and minced

2 tablespoons tomato paste

2 cups Madeira

¼ cup Crème de Menthe

1 tablespoon chopped fresh tarragon

3 tablespoons unsalted butter

GARNISH:

⅓ cup honey

⅓ cup Pommery mustard

⅓ cup bread crumbs

1 bunch parsley, chopped

- TO PREPARE THE MARINADE: In a large non-metallic dish, combine oil, garlic, mint, bay leaves and lemons.
- Marinate the lamb in the marinade for 2 days in the refrigerator, covered.
- Preheat oven to 500°F.
- TO PREPARE THE SAUCE: In a large kettle, brown reserved trimmings and bones in oil. Discard oil and cover bones with 3 quarts of cold water.
- Add celery, onions, carrots, garlic, tomato paste, Madeira, Crème de Menthe and tarragon. Heat and reduce liquid to one cup. Strain and reserve.
- Roast lamb by wrapping racks in foil and placing in oven for 8 – 10 minutes for rare to medium rare meat. Open foil. Increase heat to broil.
- TO PREPARE THE GARNISH: In a small bowl, mix mustard and honey. Spread on rack of lamb.
- Sprinkle with bread crumbs and parsley. Brown under broiler.
- Place the reduced sauce in a saucepan. Whisk in the butter. Pour sauce onto 4 warmed plates. Place the racks of lamb on the sauce after removing foil.

4 SERVINGS

Locke-Ober Cafe
Winter Place
Boston, MA. 02108

Mussels au Gratin

Legal Sea Foods, Inc.
5 Cambridge Center
Kendall Square
Cambridge, MA. 02140

GARLIC BUTTER:

3 sticks butter

¼ cup garlic, chopped

¼ cup parsley, chopped

½ teaspoon freshly ground black pepper

- TO PREPARE GARLIC BUTTER: Bring butter to room temperature.
- Mix with garlic, parsley and pepper.

MUSSELS:

12 mussels

12 ounces fresh bread crumbs

1 pound Monterey Jack cheese, grated

- Preheat oven to 400°F.
- TO PREPARE MUSSELS: Wash and scrub mussels carefully.
- Place in a large pan, cover and steam until all mussels are fully opened, approximately 7 – 10 minutes.
- Drain and remove one shell.
- Place mussels in a circle in a large heat-proof plate, one for each person.
- Using a pastry bag, pipe some garlic butter on each mussel.
- Sprinkle with cheese over the entire surface.
- Then sprinkle over with bread crumbs.
- Bake for 10 – 12 minutes or until brown and butter is bubbling.

Note: *Salt content of mussels varies greatly. Be cautious in adding salt. If using unsalted butter, ½ teaspoon salt may be used in the garlic butter.*

Boston Cream Pie with Bittersweet Chocolate Frosting

Omni Parker House
60 School Street
Boston, MA. 02108

CAKE:

2¼ cups all purpose flour

Pinch of salt

1½ teaspoons baking powder

1 cup plus 2 tablespoons unsalted butter, room temperature

1 cup granulated sugar

5 eggs, lightly beaten

1 teaspoon vanilla extract

½ – ¾ cup milk

PASTRY CREAM:

3 egg yolks

3 tablespoons granulated sugar

2½ tablespoons cornstarch

1 cup milk

1 teaspoon vanilla extract

FROSTING:

1 cup heavy cream

6 ounces bittersweet or semi-sweet chocolate, chopped

¼ cup unsalted butter, cut up

- Preheat the oven to 350°F.

- Grease two 8″ layer cake pans and dust with flour, tapping out excess.

- Sift together flour, salt and baking powder and set these aside.

- With an electric mixer, cream the butter until it is soft and light. Then add the sugar a little at a time, beating thoroughly.

- Add the eggs a spoonful at a time, beating well, then add the vanilla.

Continued on next page

Omni Parker House
60 School Street
Boston, MA. 02108

- With the mixer set at its lowest speed, add the flour to the batter alternately with the milk, taking care to mix in the flour as lightly as possible, or the cake will be too heavy.

- If necessary add another tablespoon of milk or enough to make a batter that just falls off the beaters.

- Divide the batter between the pans and spread it evenly with a rubber spatula, making the edges slightly higher than the middle, so the cakes will be level after cooking.

- Transfer the cakes to the middle of the oven and bake for 45 minutes, or until the sides of the cakes pull away slightly from the edges of the pans and the tops spring back when pressed lightly with a fingertip.

- Leave the cakes in the pans to cool slightly, then turn them out onto wire racks to cool completely.

- TO PREPARE THE PASTRY CREAM: In a bowl, whisk together the egg yolks, sugar, cornstarch and 2 tablespoons of the milk.

- In a heavy-based saucepan, bring the remaining milk to the scalding point, then whisk it, one tablespoon at a time, into the egg yolk mixture.

- Return the entire mixture to the saucepan and cook it over medium-high heat, whisking constantly, until the mixture comes to a boil.

- Lower the heat and let the mixture simmer for 1 minute.

- Remove the pastry cream from the heat and whisk in the vanilla.

- Transfer the mixture to a bowl and press a piece of plastic wrap directly onto the surface of the cream. Let it cool at room temperature.

- TO ASSEMBLE: Set the cakes on a board. Holding a serrated knife parallel to the board, cut the cakes in half horizontally, keeping the 2 sections of each cake together.

- Divide the pastry cream into thirds and using a metal palette knife, sandwich the sections with the pastry cream, then sandwich the 2 cakes together, arranging them so that the tops are sandwiched together in the middle of the assembled cake.

- Using wide metal spatulas, transfer the cake to a cake stand and tuck strips of wax paper along the bottom edge.

Continued on next page

- TO PREPARE THE FROSTING: In a heavy-based saucepan, combine the cream and chocolate and cook them over medium heat until the chocolate melts and the cream is quite hot.

- Stir the mixture with a whisk. (The chocolate may separate from the cream and turn into a mass at the bottom of the pan, but it will eventually come together to make a homogeneous mixture.)

- Remove the chocolate cream from the heat and whisk in the butter a little at a time, let each piece melt before adding another.

- Transfer the mixture to a deep bowl and set it inside a roasting pan filled with ice.

- Whisk the mixture gently until it starts to thicken. Do not leave unattended.

- When the chocolate has become spreadable, remove it from the ice and use a long metal spatula to frost the top and sides of the cake.

- Pull out the wax paper strips and set the cake aside for at least an hour to mellow.

- Cut the cake into wedges for serving.

1 CAKE

Omni Parker House
60 School Street
Boston, MA. 02108

Fruit Tart

The Ritz-Carlton, Boston
15 Arlington Street
Boston, MA. 02117

PASTRY CREAM:

1 cup milk

¼ teaspoon vanilla extract

5 teaspoons granulated sugar

3 medium size egg yolks

1 tablespoon all purpose
flour

1 tablespoon cornstarch

1 (6 ounce) pie crust or
prepared shell

1 (8 ounce) angel food cake

10 whole strawberries

1 kiwi, peeled

1 (12 ounce) jar apricot jam

- Place milk, vanilla and 5 teaspoons sugar in saucepan and bring to boil.

- In a bowl, beat egg yolks and 3½ tablespoons sugar vigorously for 1 minute using a wire whisk, until mixture begins to lighten in color.

- Sprinkle the flour and cornstarch into the bowl, carefully stirring into the egg-sugar mixture with the whisk until mixed and perfectly smooth.

- Pour half the milk mixture into the egg-sugar mixture, beating vigorously with wire whisk as milk is added.

- Pour this mixture into the remaining milk mixture, continuing to whisk.

- Place pan on high heat and boil for 1 minute, beating constantly so it does not stick, lowering the heat if necessary.

- Remove the pastry cream mixture from heat and pour into a bowl. Cool.

- To prevent a skin from forming, place a piece of plastic wrap directly on the pastry cream surface.

- Place cooled cream in pastry shell even with the edge.

- Place a thin slice of the angel cake on top of the cream.

- Slice strawberries in half. Slice kiwi in 5 – 6 pieces.

- Arrange fruit decoratively to cover entire surface of angel food cake.

- Heat jam, strain it and lightly glaze the fruit.

- Keep refrigerated until serving time.

6 – 8 SERVINGS

Note: Fresh blueberries or raspberries and/or mandarin oranges can be used.

Atlantic Shellfish Stew

STEW BASE:

2 pounds white fish bones

2 carrots, coarsely chopped

1 large onion, coarsely chopped

3 stalks celery, coarsely chopped

2 garlic cloves

¼ cup olive oil

Pinch saffron

1 quart water

1 cup white wine

GARNISH:

¼ cup olive oil

Pinch saffron

½ carrot, julienned

½ onion, julienned

½ stalk celery, julienned

½ fennel, julienned

2 garlic cloves, minced

2 fresh tomatoes, chopped

2 tablespoons brandy

2 tablespoons Pernod

¼ cup white wine

SEAFOOD:

1 lobster, 1 – 1½ pounds

2 sea scallops

2 small clams

2 mussels

2 large shrimp

- TO PREPARE THE STEW BASE: Wash bones and place in heat-proof dish with carrots, onion, celery, garlic, oil and saffron.
- Cook over medium heat, stirring constantly, for 3 – 4 minutes to reduce water content of vegetables and bones.
- Add water and wine and simmer for 20 minutes.
- Strain out solids, reserving broth.
- TO PREPARE THE GARNISH: Warm oil and saffron and add carrots, onions, celery, fennel, garlic and tomatoes.
- Sauté vegetables lightly. Add brandy and Pernod and flame.
- Add wine and simmer.
- TO PREPARE THE SEAFOOD: Split the lobster, remove claws and crack.
- Place lobster, scallops, clams, mussels and shrimp in heat-proof dish with fish broth and vegetable garnish. Heat to a boil. Reduce heat.
- Simmer for 5 minutes. Serve piping hot.

2 SERVINGS

Rowes Wharf Restaurant
Boston Harbor Hotel
70 Rowes Wharf
Boston, MA. 02110

Minced Chicken in Lettuce Leaves

Sally Ling's Restaurant
Hyatt Regency Hotel
Cambridge, MA. 02139
10 Langley Road
Newton Center, MA.
02158

MARINADE:

1 egg white	**1 teaspoon cornstarch**
¼ teaspoon salt	**1 teaspoon vegetable oil**

STIR FRY:

8 ounces white chicken meat	**½ teaspoon salt**
2 dried Chinese Black mushrooms	**1 teaspoon white wine**
5 teaspoons vegetable oil, divided	**¼ teaspoon granulated sugar**
1 teaspoon fresh chopped garlic	**1 teaspoon sesame oil**
	1 teaspoon cornstarch
	1 tablespoon water
½ cup diced celery (⅛″ dice)	**4 lettuce leaves**
½ cup diced red pepper (⅛″ dice)	**¼ cup pine nuts**

- Remove all fat from chicken, dice into ⅛″ cubes and marinate in a mixture of egg white, salt, cornstarch and vegetable oil.

- Soak dried mushrooms in hot water, cut off the stems and chop into ⅛″ cubes.

- Heat 1 tablespoon oil in wok. Add chicken and stir fry until 80 percent done. Pour it into a bowl and drain off oil.

- Heat 2 teaspoons oil in wok, add chopped garlic and stir fry for 1 minute. Add mushrooms, celery and red pepper and sauté for 1 more minute.

- Add chicken to wok with salt, wine, sugar, sesame oil and water mixed with cornstarch. Stir thoroughly.

- Cut lettuce leaves into round pieces, similar in size to a 4 – 5″ diameter bowl.

- When serving, use lettuce as a crêpe or taco to wrap the stir fry.

- Garnish with pine nuts.

4 SERVINGS

Sautéed Prawn and Scallops Shanghai Style

¾ **pound fresh shrimp, peeled**

¾ **pound fresh scallops**

1 **egg white**

1 **teaspoon cornstarch**

¾ **teaspoon salt, divided**

3 **cups plus 3 teaspoons vegetable oil, divided**

½ **cup diced onion**

½ **teaspoon chopped fresh ginger**

½ **teaspoon hot pepper sauce**

4 **teaspoons ketchup**

7 **teaspoons water, divided**

2 **teaspoons granulated sugar**

1 **teaspoon cooking wine**

Juice of 1 freshly squeezed lemon

1 **teaspoon cornstarch**

Sally Ling's Restaurant
Hyatt Regency Hotel
Cambridge, MA. 02139

10 Langley Road
Newton Center, MA.
02158

- Clean and dry shrimp and scallops with a paper towel.

- Mix together egg white, cornstarch, ¼ teaspoon salt and 1 teaspoon vegetable oil.

- Marinate shrimp and scallops in this mixture for ½ hour.

- Heat 3 cups of oil to about 300°F. in wok.

- Pour shrimp and scallops in and deep fry until they are light brown in color. Remove from oil and drain oil from wok.

- Heat 2 teaspoons oil in wok and stir fry onion and ginger.

- Add hot pepper sauce.

- Combine in a small bowl, ketchup, ½ teaspoon salt, 4 teaspoons water, sugar, wine and lemon juice, and add to wok.

- Add shrimp and scallops and boil for 1 minute.

- Combine cornstarch with 3 teaspoons water in small dish until smooth.

- Add cornstarch paste and stir thoroughly.

- Serve immediately.

4 SERVINGS

Sautéed Veal Medallions with Prosciutto and Sage

Ten Huntington Bar and Grill
The Westin Hotel at Copley Place
10 Huntington Avenue
Boston, MA. 02116

20 ounces trimmed veal loin

3 tablespoons butter

4 ounces Prosciutto, thinly sliced

2 tablespoons fresh sage, finely chopped

½ cup white wine

¼ cup heavy cream

Juice from 2 lemons

6 tablespoons butter, room temperature

Salt and freshly ground black pepper, to taste

- Slice veal into 2 ounce medallions.
- In large sauté pan, heat butter and brown veal two minutes on one side and one minute on the other, or until tender.
- Remove veal from pan and place a slice of Prosciutto on each medallion.
- Pour off remaining butter from pan and add wine and sage. Reduce by half.
- Add cream and lemon juice and reduce by one third.
- Whisk in the butter until incorporated.
- Season with salt and pepper.
- Spoon sauce over veal medallions.

4 SERVINGS

Boston Fish Pier

Haymarket

Clam Chowder (Turner Fisheries')

10 cherrystone clams

1 cup water, divided

6 quahog clams

4 ounces clarified butter

1 clove garlic, minced

1 medium onion, chopped and blanched

1 stalk celery, chopped and blanched

¼ teaspoon thyme

½ teaspoon white pepper

1 small bay leaf

½ cup all purpose flour

32 ounces clam juice*

1 large potato, diced and blanched

2 cups heavy cream

*Turner Fisheries
10 Huntington Avenue
Boston, MA. 02116*

- Wash cherrystone clams thoroughly with plenty of fresh water and a scrub brush.

- In a large pot, place clams in ½ cup water, cover tightly and steam until clams open.

- Repeat this process with quahog clams.

- Remove all clams from shells, chop coarsely and reserve broth in a separate container.*

- In the same pot, add butter and garlic, sauté 2 – 3 minutes.

- Add onions, celery, thyme, pepper and bay leaf.

- Sauté until onions are translucent.

- Add flour to make roux, stirring constantly.

- Cook over low heat for 5 minutes making sure not to brown roux.

- Slowly add clam juice, stirring constantly to avoid lumps.

- Simmer for 10 minutes. The chowder will be very thick at this point so be careful it does not burn.

- Add potatoes and cook until tender.

- Add cream and clams and bring back to a boil. Season to taste.

10 SERVINGS

* Sieve reserved clam broth through several layers of cheesecloth to be sure no sand remains. To this add enough bottled clam juice to equal 32 ounces. If fresh clams are not available substitute 12 – 14 ounces canned clams and use an additional 8 ounces of good commercial clam juice.

Hungarian Chicken

Union Club of Boston, Inc.
8 Park Street
Boston, MA. 02108

2 chicken breasts

Flour for dredging chicken

4 tablespoons clarified butter

½ cup julienned onions

½ cup sliced mushrooms

½ teaspoon chopped fresh dill or 1 teaspoon dried dill

2 tablespoons paprika

¼ cup sherry

⅓ cup chicken broth

⅓ cup light cream

- Preheat oven to 425°F.

- Dredge chicken breasts in flour.

- Heat butter in sauté pan on medium-high heat.

- Sear breasts 1½ minutes each side, remove from pan, reserving juices and bake in oven for 20 minutes.

- In reserved juices, sauté onions, mushrooms and dill over low heat until onions are soft.

- Add paprika.

- Deglaze with sherry.

- Add broth. Simmer for 1 minute.

- Add cream, stirring well to mix.

- Remove chicken breasts from oven and pour mushrooms, onions and sauce over chicken and serve.

2 SERVINGS

Ginger Bread

¾ **cup vegetable shortening**

2 cups molasses

3½ cups flour

3½ teaspoons baking soda

2 teaspoons ground ginger

4 teaspoons ground cinnamon

2 eggs

1 cup milk

- Preheat oven to 375°F. Grease one 10″ × 15″ pan.

- Whip shortening and molasses together.

- Sift flour. Combine with baking soda, ginger, cinnamon, eggs and milk, stirring to mix well.

- Add flour mixture to shortening and molasses.

- Pour into prepared pan and bake for approximately 20 minutes.

12 SERVINGS

Union Oyster House
41 Union Street
Boston, MA. 02108

ACKNOWLEDGEMENTS

The Cookbook Committee owes a special debt to those who nurtured the cookbook from dream to reality.

Bay State Design Associates, Inc.
CoVest Ltd.
Janet Seely — Winning title entry
The Junior League of Boston Board of Managers 1987-1989
Ocean Spray Cranberries, Inc.

RECIPE CONTRIBUTORS

Candace MacMillen Achtmeyer
Paula Adams
Cynthia Addeo
Barbara Alfond
Allandale Farms
Lawson Allen
Rebecca Andrews
Margie Arcand
Alison Arena
Meredith Atwood
Anne Avtges
Sarah Bailey
Sandra B. Baker
Laurie Beneski
Nancy Barnes Berkeley
Mrs. Davis Bernard
Naomi A. Biggar
Pam Boyer
Irene Bradford
Minda H. Bradley
Janice S. Brodil
Nancy N. Brown
Jane Bursma
Mrs. Daniel Bushnell
Susan Butts
Lissa Campbell
Patricia Carlan
Jan Carlson
Patricia G. Carolan
Andrea Caslione
Toni Cassis
Lynda Catlin
Joan A. Cavanaugh
Garret Chizzonite

Karen Clancy
Jennifer Clark
Frances Clotworthy
Caroline Coco
Carol Conlon
Dotty Corcoran
Doreen Donovan Corkin
Nancy Cowden
Margaret S. Cox
Andrea Craig
Carol E. Craig
Christopher Crawford
Elizabeth Crawford
Abigail Croyle
Rachael Daitch
Katie Daley
Kathy Dell'Aquila
Mrs. Allen DeSatnick
Ann Clemon DeWitt
Gwen DeWitt
Betsey Jane Dobson
Mimi Walch Doe
Janet Dolan
Marguerite Dole
Marie Donegan
Lynn D. Donovan
Maureen Donovan
Suzie Draper
Kathy Duane
Peggy Dutcher
Catherine Conway Eames
Dolores Eichar
Alice Eiseman
Louise Eiseman

Holly Elfman
Sherry Engelhardt
Gael Anna Evangelista
Patricia C. Feige
Armosa Fisher
Elaine Fleckenstein
Mrs. Colleen Florence
Heather Holmes Floyd
Katherine Cannon Fogler
Margo Friedman
Linda J. George
Donna H. Gibson
Karla Goodman
Rena N. Grandieri
Joan Mary Grandieri
Bonnie Greene
Lauren Gudonis
Debbie Haddad
Mrs. Dane F. Hahn
Karen Haitshorn
Mrs. David E. Hale
Priscilla Hall
Judith A. Halleran
Carolyn Halloran
Barbara J. Hamer
Mrs. Robert L. Hambleton
Sondra M. Hamilton
Barbara J. Haner
Carolyn Harder
Lisa Harlan
Ann Hartwell
Katie Harvey
Mrs. Michael C. Hayes
Carol Haynes

Karen R. Helliwell
Susan Hetzel
Joan Hewins
Mrs. Richard D. Hill
Susan Dunn Hill
Debbie Hoffman
Barbara Holz
Sheeran Phelps Howard
Karen Huff
Elizabeth Jacobs
Dorothy Jacobson
Terence Janericco
Cindy Johnson
Jo Lynne Johnson
Anne Jordan
Marsha Jordan
Mary Kakas
Eleanor Keasey
Harriet Clewis Kinnett
Barbara Ellis Kline
Diane D. Knight
Peabody Kohler
Helen Kosokowski
Mary M. Kuhrtz
Virginia D. Ladd
Mrs. Janelle D. Landrigan
Liz Larson
Ann C. Leggat
Nance H. R. Lehman
Suzanne H. Levy
Gina Graves Lloyd
Beverly Lochridge
Johanna C. Lockhart
Jane Davenport Lucas
Claire M. Luse
Ann Marie Lynch
Patricia M. Lynch
Barbara Lyons
Heidi Maddrix
Bridget Maloney
Lauren Gianelli Martens
Jean L. Martin
Lynn Stevenson McKenna
Phyllis B. Meisel
Mrs. Glenn A. Menard
Darby Denton Mengel
Paula M. Meridan
Nancy Miles
Judy Mittleman
Skye M. Morrison
Carolyn Ann Morrisey

Jinn F. Murphy
Susie Murray
Kathleen Nakushian
Mrs. Robert P. Neilson
Susie Nichols
Marcia Norcia
Mrs. Chester Norris
Pamela S. Nugent
Elizabeth O'Conor
Gayle Osborn
Laurie McDowell Osgood
Rose Marie Van Otterloo
Anne Ouellette
Kathleen Owen
Leila Parke
Gina Parker
Hilda Parrot
Elizabeth Patterson
Cynthia D. Payne
Mrs. James Pennington
Andrea Perry
Virginia Perry
Ana Peterkin
Lyn Pohl
Marilyn Pond
Mrs. James L. Pool
Melissa A. Raleigh
Alice Ridgeway
Rowan Riley
Sandra Robertson
Penny Rosebrough
Tracy Rubin
Suzanne Jaques Runton
Laurie F. Russell
Karen W. Sacchetti
Ann Sargent
Nancy Sawyer
Mrs. Richard Scheide
Carol D. Schmidt
Patricia Schoeck
Janet Seeley
Jeanne Shaughnessy
Mrs. Bruce P. Shaw
Katherine Shisler
Llnda Silva
Cynthia H. Smithy
Marlene Snider
Debra L. Snow
Ann Soloman
Mrs. Robert E. Spoerl
Jill B. Staniar

Lisa Stevens
Marian McBride-Stevens
Sharron Stolle
Aleece Strachan
Suzanne Strouse
Karen M. Sullivan
Mary Sullivan
Randi H. Sullivan
Margie Sunderland
Meg Sweeting
Linda Lewis Sylvester
Liz Taggart
Peggy Tambke
Joyce Taylor
Jaclyn W. Thayer
Patricia Anne Thomas
Jill M. Thompson
Liza Thompson
Cathy W. Tierney
Laurie Title
Gail Tomlak
Marsha Tucker
Barbara Upton
Michele Urbancic
Ann B. Vanderhoef
Susan Viano
Melissa Vokey
Julie F. Wade
Elizabeth Walker
Mary Walker
Mary Ann Walter
Mildred Lee Ward
Cornelia Sise Waring
Marcia Webb
Margaret Webb
Nancy Weber
Ellen K. Whitenight
Neila Whitbeck
Mrs. Richard Whitney
Holly Wiedemann-van Dissel
Nina Smiley Wilkins
Carol Hillsdale Williams
Debra Williams
Peggy Williamson
Lisa Wilson
Sarah Grove Wilsterman
Marian Wood
Judy Wright
Mrs. Robert D. Wyatt
M. Paige Yates

Index

Notes

Notes